China is perfectly positioned today to be the world leader in the remainder of the 21st century. The formula for China's future prosperity is very simple. All China has to do is follow the historical example of how America became very prosperous due to world events in the 20th century that America was smart enough and lucky enough to capitalize on. It can be repeated in China in this century.

East Meets West

Why China Has a Bright Economic Future and Will Be the World Leader in the 21st Century

东西相遇

为何中国经济前景光明且将成为21世纪全球领袖

Combined English and Chinese Versions
英汉对译本

By

Frank Silva

Translated into Mandarin Chinese by

卢秀娟（译）

SHOESTRING VENTURES, LLC

PUBLISHED BY: Frank Silva and Shoestring Ventures, LLC; Copyright 2012 by Frank Silva and Shoestring Ventures LLC – ISBN-10:1495398447

License Notes

This book is the intellectual property of Frank Silva and is copyrighted by Frank Silva and Shoestring Ventures, LLC. It is printed and licensed for your personal enjoyment only. If you have purchased this book from an unauthorized source or printer, please report this to shoestringventuresllc@gmail.com.

If you read this book and enjoy it and wish to share it, I am honored by that, but please also encourage others to purchase a copy for themselves.

Author's Personal Note:

The contents of this book, all thoughts and ideas within, are my intellectual property that I have generously chosen to share with you, all readers, and especially the people of China. I hope the content helps you greatly and contributes to your future prosperity. If you pay for this book in either the digital or print version, the god of fortune will reward you beyond your wildest imagination and your prosperity will be unlimited. If you download this book without paying for it, or obtain an unauthorized printed version, a ghost will haunt you each night as you sleep. I have a great respect for Chinese people and believe that Chinese people have a deep sense of honor and a rich culture, and the vast majority will do the right thing and purchase a copy of the book, in ebook or print version, if they want to read it, rather than stealing a copy without paying for it. Thank you for respecting my hard work, thank you for your support and good luck in your future endeavors in this exciting time in China.

出版发行：
Frank Silva and Shoestring Ventures LLC
Copyright 2012 by Frank Silva and Shoestring
Ventures LLC – ISBN-13: 978-1495398445

授权说明

此书是 Frank Silva 的个人著作，版权归 Frank Silva and Shoestring Ventures, LLC 所有，仅供个人阅读之用。如从任何未授权途径或非法书商购得此书，请以电邮形式告知，电邮地址：shoestringventuresllc@gmail.com。

如果你读了这本书，喜欢这本书并且希望与别人分享这本书，我感到很荣幸，但是也请你鼓励你的朋友购买一本。

作者的话：

我在这里慷慨地与所有读者，特别是中国读者，分享此书包含的所有想法和观点，这些都是我个人智慧的结晶。我希望这些内容能够对你们未来实现繁荣富强有所帮助。如果你从正式途径购买了此书的电子版或者印刷版，财富之神将给予你超乎想像的、永无止境的财富；如果你不花一分钱下载了这本书，或者从非法途径得到此书的印刷版，你将彻夜难眠，夜夜受鬼怪缠扰。我非常尊重中国人民，我相信中国人尊重劳动成果，拥有灿烂的文化，大部分人还是会做正确的事情，如果他们想阅读此书，他们会购买正版的电子版或者印刷版，而不会免费下载或购买盗版。谢谢你们对我辛勤劳动的尊重，谢谢你们的支持，但愿你们在这激动人心的时代里靠自身努力过上美好的生活

This work is dedicated to my Chinese friends, Chinese businesspeople, and Chinese students of English wherever they may be. This is also for the working class people of the world who struggle daily to survive in an environment where the privileged or lucky gain the lion's share of rewards, and all the advantages that money and privilege affords. May the future bring us fairer, better and more equitable ways where intelligence, talent and creativity win over power, wealth, privilege or unfair advantages. We are all in this together. The best of the best should rise and lift everyone else with them.

For the people of China, your future is indeed bright. And you should prosper greatly from the information contained within this book. If you do, that will make me happy. It will make me happier if you give me 10%.

****

Those who hear not the music think the dancers mad. - Anonymous

谨以此书献给我的中国朋友们、中国商人们以及所有学英语的中国学生们,无论他们身在何方。我还想献给世界上那些苦苦挣扎的打工一族,我们生活在一个不公平的社会,少部分幸运的有权有势的人掌握了极大部分的社会财富以及金钱和权力换来的好处。但愿未来的社会变得更好,更公平,财富分配更公正,人的知识、天赋和创造力比权力、财富、特权和不公平的优势更重要。让我们一起努力,这些少数幸运的人应该带领大多数人一起过上更美好的生活。

对于中国人来说,你们的前途一片光明。你们应该利用这本书提供的信息最大程度地繁荣兴旺起来。如果你们真的因为看了这本书而变得富有起来,我会非常高兴。如果你们可以给我你们财富的百分之十,我会更加高兴,呵呵。

****

那些听不见音乐的人觉得舞者是疯子。— 佚名

EAST MEETS WEST

*****

This book is not about politics or political ideology. It's not about Capitalism versus Communism. It's not about the cultural differences between America and China. It's not about great empires or powerful nations and how they rise or fall.

It's not even about the hybrid system of business practiced by China today, which is a Communist country that is practicing Capitalism better than America, a nation which by all accounts in the world is the leading capitalist country and most successful capitalist country in the history of the world. Although the hybrid system practiced by China, which can be called capitacommunism, might be a factor in any discussion today of world finance and economics.

Additionally, there are many books today, written by prominent authors, businessmen and economists, about business in China, about doing business in China, about doing business with China, Chinese companies and in Chinese factories. There are also many other books about various aspects of business management or economics and how they apply to China, as if China is on another planet far from the Western world. One author's 2001 book even suggested that China's economy would collapse in 2006. I can't be sure, but as I write this in 2012, I think he was wrong. Wait, let me look out the window. Yes, he was wrong.

Regardless of the thoughts or comparisons above, or my little joke about the well-respected but very wrong author, or the factors, discussion and examples contributing to my analysis and predictions about China's future, this book is purely about business and history.

More specifically, it is about business in the 20th century in America and how America became a dominant business leader in the world. It is about the history of how that happened. It is about history that, many times in the world, repeats itself at different times in different places. It is about how it is China's turn to be a world leader and how that will probably come to be, in this century, sooner rather than later.

I would be lying if I did not say that as an American it saddens me greatly to see the decline of my great country. I am equally disheartened by some of the choices my country has made in recent years, especially after the events of 9/11. However, as a student of history, it will be interesting and exciting to witness the rise of China as an economic power in the world.

Keep in mind that the ideas of dominance or influence or global power of nations do not interest me. Those are political ideologies. I'm not writing about political ideologies. I'm interested in our world and the people in it. The world is abundant and there is enough of everything we need for all people (and all nations). On a global scale we just need the world's ultra-wealthy and political leaders to stop acting like spoiled little boys in the school yard and start acting like adults that have genuine concern for our planet and all its people, as well as the environment and the other living things in our world.

There is a story in America about a U.S. astronaut on his first time orbiting the earth in space. It takes a space capsule ninety minutes to orbit the earth. This astronaut said that on his first day he would look out the window every hour and a half, when he was over his hometown. Then he looked only at his state; then the area of the country where he lived. Then he looked at the United States. And within a couple of days he only saw the world as a whole.

When I first heard that story I said that it would be great if we could take every world leader and put them in space, orbiting the earth, for just five days. Maybe the world would change for the better.

I would suggest that we also do this with the world's ultra-wealthy. However, I believe most of them would only see the world as their property or a place to conquer and dominate with their wealth, rather than a home occupied and shared by all people.

In the absence of the possibility of sending any leaders to space, we have what we have in our world.

It saddens me that the conditions that created America's great Middle Class and that contributed to America's prosperity in the 20th century were purposely dismantled by the greedy ultra-wealthy and the corporations that they own. That was devastating to the American economy and the working and middle classes.

However, it is great for China and the Chinese people. It is part of what made China the prosperous nation that it is today and what will transform China into a world leader in the near future.

The key is that China *has* many people.

China, unfortunately, also has many poor people.

On a scale compared to America, that problem may not be easy to solve. America today, I believe, has as many, or more, poor people than China. The difference is that in America we only have 300 million people, so the number of poor people will be much less by comparison than China's 1.4 billion people.

Aside from that, the number of people in China will be a key factor in China's rise in prosperity and rise as a global economic power.

Taking the number of people into account, as both labor and consumers, it is easy to see the direction China is going in the future.

The history of America in the 20th century will show us the most likely path that China is on in the 21st century. And that path will lead to prosperity for China and the majority of Chinese people who are conscientious, hard workers, striving each day to make a better life for themselves and their loved ones.

I'm not saying I have all the answers here. But I do believe that this is good information and essential information that people engaging in business in China or that savvy Chinese business leaders can use as a road map to future prosperity.

I would also like you to keep in mind that as I write this in 2012, the world is relatively stable. I believe this is the path China will take in its future, barring anything unusual happening in the world, such as a major world war or worldwide environmental catastrophe, a pandemic or an economic meltdown that impacts on every nation including China.

Absent of these or other disasters, what follows is China's most likely path to greater prosperity and global leadership.

Passing the Baton

In a relay race, the runner passing the baton bears down on the next runner. The next runner, waiting for his turn in the race, anticipates the speed of his teammate and begins to sprint while glancing back over his shoulder and extending his hand, palm up, behind him, in expectation that his teammate will catch up to him, and place the baton in his hand. That runner then becomes the main competitor in the race for his part of the race.

We can compare this to the rise and fall of the many powerful empires in history. Many of those empires, full of confidence and feeling invincible, became arrogant and self-destructive. Unfortunately, many of those empires, drunk on power, have also done many dishonorable things in the world in their attempts to maintain power.

Regardless of that, the fact is that a simple search of history will show the great empires and tell when and how they declined and handed power to the empire that followed it.

Rome, for example, was one of the great Empires in world history. The Roman Empire had technological marvels unprecedented in their day, such as roads, bridges, aqueducts and sewers. But its empire declined and it no longer exists today. And unfortunately today there are many similarities between Ancient Rome and modern America.

In modern times, many European countries fought for dominance and control, each taking turns as the world leader. (The world as they knew it.) Countries such as Spain and France were at times very powerful, very wealthy and very influential in the world. For this book I only need to go back to the 19th century when Britain "ruled" the world.

In recent history Great Britain and its empire was the most prosperous and most influential nation on earth. Chinese people will remember that Hong Kong was a British colony and the Brits were very influential in cities such as Shanghai.

Great Britain was clearly the dominant country in the world. And even after losing its great colonies in the American Revolution, it was still the world leader at the time. (By the way, the American Revolution would not have been successful without the help of France, one of England's biggest historical rivals and for that I will always be grateful to France and the French people and Americans today still owe a great debt to France. Without France the United States would not exist. Far too many Americans overlook that in favor of remembering how America liberated France in 20th century world wars.)

By the end of the 19th century, however, Great Britain was overextended and could not sustain its empire. It was spending too much money. Many of its colonies were starting to seek independence. The final nail in the coffin came from the expense of World War I in the early 20th century.

After World War I the baton started to pass to the United States. Despite the Great Depression, the U.S. continued to be the rising world power. For a few years Great Britain and the U.S. worked very closely and in some cases, such as in the Middle East, both countries shared power, but it was clear that Britain was declining and America was rising. World War II and the Allied Victory, along with the U.S. developing an atomic bomb, pushed America into the number one spot as the unquestioned world leader.

The United States has been the dominant country in the world since then. In fact, as I write this, the United States is still the dominant nation in the world. However, I believe that is about to change and the baton will pass to China in the 21st century. No one can predict exactly when this will happen, but it is my guess that it has already started and will happen within the next ten to twenty years.

Here's the first secret I'll tell you in this book: China doesn't need the West. Western countries need China. China does not need the help of any country to rise to a leader in the world. China can be self-sufficient and independent and prosperous beyond what anyone can imagine today. Many Chinese people claim that the West has better technology and therefore an advantage in business and economics. That might be true in 2012. But there are intelligent, creative and innovative people everywhere. America, or anywhere else in the West, does not have a monopoly on those traits. The West and America might have a slight advantage, from both an historical view and a technological view, but that's changing and new research is being done on new technology almost everywhere in the world today. China's distinct advantages today, in size, population, resources and manufacturing gives it bigger advantages over America in decline and Western nations suffering economic hardships.

The China runner, in my example of a world relay race, has started taking his first steps, he is speeding up and he is anxiously awaiting for the baton to be passed to him.

FRANK SILVA

Building a Consumer Society

Building a consumer society, as America did, can be a great benefit to a nation.

Consumers, as well as exports, drive the economy of any nation. Consumption provides jobs and manufacturing and income for workers who then go out and spend that income on products and services that consumers need or want. Remember, consumers will choose to spend their money on things they need to survive and things they want that make them happy.

The consumer society in America made our economy grow. It made our working class prosper and it built our large middle class.

Consumption is not a bad thing. However, extreme consumption is bad and possibly destructive. The trick is to have healthy consumption that grows and sustains an economy, without moving into a destructive stage of over consumption. It can be done, but it takes guidance from economic experts and education of consumers to make good choices in their buying and consuming habits.

I believe America passed the productive stage of prosperous consumption and went beyond it to the stage of extreme consumption which is very destructive. I don't blame this fully on the American people, however. I blame it on the corporations that are always in pursuit of higher sales and more profits and banks that are always willing to lend money that put people in lifetime debt.

These factors, I believe, lead to destructive consumption. What's most destructive is the combination of corporations constantly pursuing higher sales and revenue and a culture taught by the bankers that instant gratification is worth personal debt.

Most middle class homes in America have garages. In America today, however, few cars are kept in the garage. The garage is used as a storage area for the many "things" that Americans buy, that are replaced by other new things and there is no room left in the house for the old things. Many Americans have garages full of things they don't use or need or want anymore and many more Americans have many more things in public storage units. Private companies that provide nothing but garage-like storage areas that can be locked and are protected by the storage company are very big business in America. As crazy as it sounds, storage companies are everywhere in America and many of them are full with few units vacant. People pay rent every month to store things they've accumulated that they no longer use, but can't bring themselves to get rid of by either selling them or throwing them away.

In addition, every summer, many families and neighborhoods have garage sales where people put all their unwanted things on their lawn and sell them to other people. Sometimes people can get great bargains at garage sales for many things they might need or want and sometimes they just get rid of some things and buy other things from someone else's garage. More often than not, people end up selling some things they don't want anymore, but they replace them with things they buy from someone else who doesn't want them anymore. Then they go home and replace the things in their house with these *new* old things and put the things in their house into the garage. It sounds crazy and it sounds like I'm trying to be funny, and partly I am, but it's true.

Over consumption also includes food and has also led to Americans being the fattest people on earth, and this has already proven to be very destructive in many ways, from higher healthcare costs to early death.

**

Healthy consumerism drives an economy and, in China's case, it will be what makes China continue to grow and prosper. Healthy consumerism keeps people working and allows people to buy the things they want or need, like different types of clothes, cell phones, music, computers, home appliances and everything else that makes life more comfortable and raises the standard of living of people and families.

And with 1.4 billion consumers, China's economy can grow larger and faster than any Western nation in history.

Business and Growth

There are many factors involved in economic growth.

I don't intend to explain all of them here or make this a college course in economics. I'm attempting to make a practical guide that Chinese business leaders and entrepreneurs can use to make good decisions and to be successful and make better lives for themselves and their families.

With that in mind, every business wants to grow. Growth is essential to increased profits and prosperity.

However, there is usually a limit to everything.

Here is a perfect example to consider about growth and limits taken from the American fast food industry.

Before I explain this concept I will apologize from the American people for bringing McDonald's, KFC and Pizza Hut to China. They may be popular and some of their products may be somewhat delicious, but just as they have contributed to obesity, diabetes, heart disease and unhealthy lifestyles in America, as I said above, they are doing the same to Chinese people today. In addition, pizza is one of my favorite foods and can be healthy if eaten in moderation. However, Pizza Hut, even in America, can hardly be called pizza. Some people in America, people like me that value nutritious food and who aren't stupid enough to fall for clever or deceptive advertising, wouldn't feed McDonald's or Pizza Hut to a dog.

But enough of what I think of the taste or lack of nutritional value of fast food.

**

When the American fast food industry was created shortly after World War II, it was a brilliant business concept.

The founders of these businesses had the idea that their one restaurant could be replicated, ensuring that the food and service was identical in each.

The idea was that if people liked the food in a particular restaurant in New York, they could get the very same food, such as a hamburger, in the same restaurant in Miami or Los Angeles or any other city.

This idea became popular and the fast food chains built themselves into large nationwide companies.

The fast food industry became very competitive. In America we have many fast food restaurants. McDonald's has been the leader in fast food since it started in America. But it has been challenged by other restaurants such as Burger King and Wendy's and many other Western brands that China does not have.

The companies all grew to well-known brand names operating nationwide.

That's when the fun started, and in their attempts to gain market share and steal customers from each other, these companies tried many different strategies. Most of these strategies worked and they all started doing the same things in fierce competition.

For example: One restaurant offered a meal for children and it came with a little toy. So the other companies had to do the same. Then one company would sign a business deal with a popular children's movie or TV show and would offer the movie or TV characters as stuffed-doll toys with the meal. So the frenzy started with each company trying to partner with famous and popular cartoon characters or movie and TV characters so that parents would bring their kids in for a meal and get the toys as a bonus.

Specific marketing strategy aside, I want you to focus on the concept of growth in this very competitive market.

At first, these fast food restaurants offered lunch and dinner. Fast food lunch, while people were at work, was a huge market. Dinner was a much smaller market since many people went home and ate dinner with their families.

Because of the fast-paced lives that Americans lead and because more women were working instead of staying home as housewives, women had less time to prepare dinner. That's when fast food dinners started to become popular in America.

The fast food industry grew steadily on sales of lunch and dinner.

Once they started to reach their upper limit on sales for lunch and dinner they had to find something new to increase revenue. There are only so many customers and two meals, lunch and dinner.

That's when someone invented the idea of the supersize. Now, instead of just the meal, you can supersize your meal and get a bigger hamburger, bigger order of French fries and a bigger drink for a small price increase that most customers were willing to pay.

Soon, supersize became the typical meal.

The restaurants again reached their upper limit of growth.

To continue to grow they added breakfast. A whole new meal and a new market of customers.

I'm not really sure which came first, breakfast or the supersize, but it doesn't really matter. Both were strategies designed to increase sales and contribute to growth.

The competition was very strong for breakfast also, just as it became for lunch and dinner. All the companies prospered as more and more people had a fast food breakfast on the way to work or school. Many also had a fast food lunch.

Fast food was convenient, it save time and effort finding meals, and it was somewhat low cost, depending on what people bought or how much food they ate.

Soon enough, the limit was reached once again and even though all the companies continued to prosper and made billions of dollars each year, even with strong competition, they needed to invent something new in order to continue growing.

Recently I read the new marketing strategy for growth in the fast food industry. And it too is one of the things that saddens me about my country and shows how corporations and business dominates our culture.

With the upper limit reached in fast food sales, and nowhere else to go, the fast food industry is now trying to push the concept of a "fourth meal" on the American public.

Traditionally in our culture, and in most of the world, we have three meals - breakfast, lunch and dinner. In order to continue to grow, executives in the fast food industry are attempting to *re-educate* Americans and especially American children to the concept of a fourth meal to be eaten after dinner and sometime before bedtime.

Four meals a day is a ridiculous idea, but if marketing experts have their way - and they usually do - American children will grow up believing that a fourth meal is a good idea and normal. In time it will be seen as something we've always done in our society and a typical eating habit in our culture.

I see it as another case of consumerism gone wrong and how the influence of businesses to gain profits can be destructive.

People don't need four meals a day. Many don't get three. Some barely get two. And many people are lucky to get any food at all.

However, the point is that in order to continue to grow, the fast food industry had nowhere else to go, so they invented a new market.

**

To relate this to China - the consumer market in China, for any product or service, is

1.4 billion customers. China has not yet begun to tap into that large consumer market. China is in its infancy as a consumer society.

Due to that, the potential growth for most products and services is virtually unlimited today. This is what will drive China's impressive increase in prosperity, while raising the standard of living for most Chinese people and contributing to China's rise as a world leader. And remember, even moderate sales in China's large consumer market has the potential to be three or four times more than the American consumer market during its most prosperous years.

Culture, Languages and their Influence in the World, and American Hegemony

Why does most of the world speak English? Why do so many Chinese people learn English?

I know many Chinese people that learn English because China is the world's factory and many foreign customers do business in English.

The three most-spoken languages on earth are Chinese, English and Spanish.

It's easy to see why Chinese is an important language spoken by many people.

Studying history also reveals why Spanish is a prominent language.

When Spain had a great empire it colonized many lands and islands in the New World. Those lands and islands formed new nations and due to that, most of those nations in Central and South America and Mexico in North America, speak Spanish.

Due to the many immigrants in the United States that come from the Latin American countries, a large percentage of people in the U.S. speak Spanish. Experts estimate that sometime in the middle of this century there will be more Spanish speaking people in America than people speaking English.

Portugal sent explorers sailing to the New World also and the largest nation in South America - Brazil - speaks Portuguese. Brazil is a large trading country with Chinese factories and yet Chinese factories and Brazilian customers do business in English.

Why?

The British had a great empire before the United States rose to prominence in the world in the 20th century. The British colonized many parts of the world and many parts of Asia. English was taught to many Asian people.

However, what made English the dominant language in the world, especially for business purposes, was America's rise to power after World War II. (As a side note, America's power also allowed it to ensure that the U.S. Dollar became the world's reserve currency. However, due to the financial problems in the U.S., especially the financial meltdown in 2008, many nations are looking to replace the world's reserve currency to a basket of currencies, and in addition, some nations are now trading directly in their own currencies rather than in U.S. Dollars.)

The influence of English in global business will not change any time soon.

However, I believe that in this century, Chinese will become a much more important global language. Spanish will be important because many people speak it. But for global commerce and dominant influence in the world, Chinese and English will compete as prominent languages in this century.

Many people in Europe speak multiple languages. Europe is a relatively small area for the number of countries it has. Due to trade and travel it was only smart for Europeans to learn many languages.

For various reasons Americans are largely ignorant of foreign cultures and foreign languages. Part of the arrogance of empires that I mentioned earlier is to blame for this.

FRANK SILVA

Throughout most of the 20th century, Americans felt that since we were the envy of the world, and the leader of the world, that many people would learn our language.

That was true. But due to that, Americans stopped learning about other cultures or other languages. Americans today are only beginning to realize this mistake. Few, however, are attempting to do anything to change it.

The important thing to remember about this as we go further into the 21st century, is that anyone, especially those engaging in business anywhere, will have a great advantage if they speak Chinese or English. And anyone speaking Chinese *and* English will be way ahead of everyone else and can operate at a much greater advantage. And people that speak Chinese, English and Spanish will be able to do almost anything on earth.

(I left out Arabic, although it is an important language today. Many Middle Eastern nations speak Arabic and although the world is very small and getting smaller each day, I believe that with the coming end of oil most of the Middle East nations will be unimportant and will be left powerless in the years to come. I believe that if Western or Asian nations leave them alone, they will do the same. And therefore Arabic will not be a much needed language and certainly not nearly as important as Chinese, English and Spanish. The only other language that could be of importance is Russian, but that would depend on Russia's future position in the world.)

A Short History of America's Rise to Power

Great Britain started to lose its power towards the end of the 19th century. Its empire was overextended, much like the empires in history before it. In addition, many of its colonies wanted to be free and independent. This happened at the same time that America began to rise as a world power due to its expansion beyond its continental borders.

World War I, for all practical purposes, bankrupted Britain. At the same time, America held off entering the war while preparing for it. When America entered the war it was ready to win and with America's help Germany was defeated.

At this time in history, new inventions, such as planes and tanks, started to influence how wars were fought and because of that, oil became very important.

Due to the amount of oil in the Middle East, that area of the world also became a very important and strategic location. And as England started to decline, the United States started to gain more power in the Middle East. For a short period of time the U.S. and Great Britain worked closely to control the countries and resources there.

One of the problems existing today began at that time. The borders of Iraq were defined by Great Britain. The problem was that this country contained three main cultures of people, Sunni Muslims, Shiite Muslims and Kurds.

The Shiite Muslims were the largest majority, while the Kurds were second. The Western powers of Great Britain and the U.S., however, struck a business deal with the Sunni Muslims. In exchange for low-cost oil, the two nations would support a government of Iraq controlled by the minority Sunni Muslims and even though they were the minority they would be protected by the military power of both Great Britain and the United States.

This is just one of the problems that the politics of oil has caused in the world.

Since many prominent and prosperous Americans came out of World War I even more prosperous and powerful, they started to influence the world economy and other world events.

This led to what was called the "roaring twenties" in America, which was the period of time during the 1920s. During this time businesses owned by the wealthiest Americans started to exercise their influence backed by U.S. power. Banks and businesses were building rapidly and stocks were being traded on Wall Street to new and increasing levels.

American businesses were operating with little government interference. Many wealthy people became even wealthier.

However, unregulated business practices in the U.S., along with unethical behavior on the part of the large companies in America, led the world to the stock market crash of 1929.

This marked the beginning of the Great Depression and the U.S. and world economy got even worse from 1929 to 1933.

In the 1930s, U.S. president Franklin Delano Roosevelt had the government pass more laws to regulate businesses so that they could not be so destructive to our national economy. He also used tax-payer-funded government initiatives to invest in our nation and try to bring our nation and people out of the severe poverty it was in due to the Great Depression.

During this time, we built new roads, bridges and other parts of our national infrastructure. He also started Social Security so that working people would have a regular income after retirement and be secure in their old age.

America made a little progress in the 1930s but the Great Depression made a deep impact. We had many poor, homeless and jobless people.

America's influential business owners and politicians knew, however, by the mid 1930s that a new war was on the horizon.

No one likes war. War is expensive to the tax payers that fund it, it is destructive and it kills many people. And the people that die are usually the innocent ones. Unfortunately, the powerful and wealthy people profit from war and they are the ones that continue to promote them and start news ones. Corporations and their wealthy owners are the only ones that like war, because they make very high profits in total safety, far away from the death and destruction.

America's strategy again, during the 1930s, similar to World War I, was to wait as long as possible before entering any war that started, while simultaneously preparing for war and positioning American industries to profit greatly from war. (As a side note in America, during World War II some wealthy people performed military service, during Vietnam the vast majority of wealthy people avoided military service, including George W. Bush, and today, *no* wealthy people bother to perform any service that they all largely praise as being a "patriotic" duty.)

Despite the facts that war had been going on in the Pacific, with Japan already invading countries such as China, and with the official start of World War II in September of 1939 when Germany invaded Poland, the United States waited until it was fully prepared to enter the war.

In fact, future president Harry Truman, at the time a U.S. Senator, said that America should wait as long as possible and see who is winning (between Germany and Russia) before joining the war so that each country can kill as many people as possible before the U.S. got involved.

The American leadership and war strategists finally chose sides and made plans to enter the war. The easiest way to do this was to put Japan in a position that would force it to attack the United States. (Although we have had continuous and ongoing wars for most of our history, in U.S. culture we like to fool ourselves into believing we are a nation of peace and aside from recent events in the Middle East and Central Asian nations where we are the aggressor, we try to force other nations to attack us first so we can claim the moral high ground and believe we have a good reason to "retaliate" or attack them for their "aggression".)

Even though we were not yet at war with the Axis powers of Germany, Italy and

Japan, the United States did everything possible to cut Japan off from its much-needed supplies of oil. That put Japan in a position of running out of oil and therefore losing the war, or attacking the U.S. to try to obtain oil.

I will not go into an entire history of World War II. We all know the result.

The only thing I will mention is that America got very lucky in developing the atomic bomb before Germany. If Germany had developed it first, the war would have had a very different outcome and it would not have been good for either the United States or China.

**

What happened *after* World War II is what is important to China and may very well be a blueprint to China's rise to prosperity and power in the 21st century.

At the end of World War II, much of Europe was destroyed. Most, if not all, of the factories in Germany were destroyed and many cities were as well.

At this time in history, Asian countries, and China in particular, were very underdeveloped and had little new technology.

By default the United States, which had its factories working overtime producing all the materials and products needed for the war, became the world's factory. The U.S. stopped most of its wartime manufacturing and converted back to making consumer products. During the war, for example, car factories stopped making cars and made jeeps, tanks and planes instead. After the war the factories went back to manufacturing cars.

This next part of American history is the important part for Chinese people to focus on.

America was manufacturing products for export to the world. Americans were employed and working full time with rising wages due to rising sales and rising corporate profits. With more money, Americans started to demand more consumer products.

Americans working in one factory were making products, not only for export to the world markets, but for sale to Americans working in other American factories.

This cycle continued and increased the standard of living in America. It pushed many working class Americans into incomes that put them solidly in the American Middle Class. Our middle class increased significantly and our nation and people prospered greatly. We became a much wealthier nation - and by "much wealthier nation" I mean working class and middle class people as well as the corporations that were happily increasing revenue and profits very much also during this time of prosperity.

This continued through the 1950s when Americans were very prosperous and very happy.

From a business perspective the 1960s were a very profitable decade, but also one that was marred by social unrest in America. America's involvement in Vietnam along with both black people and women speaking up for their rights, two groups that were (and still are) widely discriminated against in our culture, contributed to a very difficult decade in America. We also had a president assassinated in 1963 - John F. Kennedy. Later in the decade, in 1968, his brother Bobby Kennedy, while running for president, was also assassinated. In the same year, America's great Civil Rights leader, who spoke out for equality for black people and an end to the war in Vietnam, Martin Luther King Jr., was also assassinated. By contrast, American astronauts also walked on the moon in 1969.

It was a very difficult, exciting and dynamic decade that in many ways changed the course of America.

During this time more women started working also. More women were in the workforce partly because they wanted more independence and partly because, in the case of families, a single income was not enough anymore.

America was still prosperous, but other nations, such as Japan started manufacturing and exporting more products.

Since American wages were continuing to rise and foreign wages were low, products made in Japan and imported to America could be sold for less and it started to make an impact on American manufactured products.

In terms of our economy, the 1970s were the turning point for America and particularly for American workers.

In the 1970s, costs for raw materials and manufacturing continued to rise along with increases in energy prices. Corporations continued to make profits. Corporations also continued raising prices to keep up with cost increases. However, corporations started to stall wages, and income for workers did not rise at the same ratio as costs, prices and profits.

American workers no longer made enough money to pay the bills and buy all the consumer goods and services they needed and wanted.

The standard of living was very high in America and products that made life more convenient became typical in our culture. Americans didn't want to give up any of these conveniences.

Rather than buy less products or lower their standard of living, banks started offering more credit and easier credit, so, American workers starting living on borrowed money and credit cards. The idea, pushed by a corporate agenda of promoting consumerism, was that Americans can easily get today anything they want and conveniently pay for it over time. What wasn't stressed to American consumers was that the banks charged interest fees and the interest fees over time greatly increased the price of consumer items like televisions, or kitchen appliances such as toaster-ovens and blenders, and all those other things that made life more comfortable.

Americans started the routine habit of buying products on credit and the credit card companies working with the banks were only too happy to provide more and more credit. The debt built up during the 1970s, and by the 1980s many Americans were drowning in debt.

Additionally, even though we have minimum wage laws, American workers could not keep up with mounting debt.

When minimum wage started it was supposed to be designed around the poverty level. Poverty level is the minimum amount of money that someone working full time would need to live, by paying monthly bills for things such as housing, food, clothes, transportation and medical care if needed. In America, when minimum wage was instituted it was supposed to be with this theory in mind, but as prices and costs continued to rise and profits for companies continued rising, minimum wage did not keep pace and did not rise along with the others. Today, for example, minimum wage is right around $7 U.S. dollars per hour, while economists have said that it should be at least $18 to $20 USD if it rose equally over the years with the other categories.

To make matters worse (for Americans), China opened up to foreign companies, especially American corporations, all of which claim to love America but hide their money in foreign countries and manipulate our laws so that they pay no U.S. taxes. And purely for business reasons, American companies moved their factories to China, despite the negative effects this would have on America and American workers.

This was very good for China and Chinese workers. Unfortunately for Chinese workers, the wages were very low. This is why the companies moved in the first place. These companies saw the opportunity to exploit the many people in China that wanted jobs and would be happy to work for almost nothing. And *almost nothing* is what American companies are usually willing to pay, with *nothing* being what they would prefer to pay if they could get away with it. (Unfortunately for them, most countries have outlawed slavery.)

This was all very bad for American workers because they saw their factories close and relocate to China (and, also at the time, Mexico).

The problem was that American workers continued living on credit and what little savings they were able to put in the bank from the years of post-World-War II prosperity.

For the American workers in the 1970s this caused them to deplete their savings and borrow more money from the banks. It also increased their use of credit cards and put them in even more debt. That increasing debt continued to drive the consumer society for another fifteen to twenty years. However, that started to become a problem in the 1990s and a much bigger problem in the new century.

In the 1980s, more and more American jobs moved to China and other countries.

In their quest for increased profits, the ultra-wealthy in America and the corporations they own, moved out of America, closing factories and putting Americans out of work. They moved to China at the expense of the American working class and middle class. They cared nothing about their country and they still don't today. They care only about profits for themselves and their corporations. (And in America these corporations avoid paying taxes of any type, even taxes for things that the ultra-wealthy and the corporations directly use or benefit from.)

Sometime during the 1990s American corporations started to really influence international business. Corporate lobbyists bought our government fully and instead of our government making laws, the corporations, through their lobbyists, were writing the laws themselves.

This led to much higher profits for corporations and the very wealthy people that own them and the very wealthy people that can invest in them. In addition they had laws passed allowing both the ultra-wealthy and the corporations to pay much lower taxes. Some giant international companies, such as GE, for example, pay only 2% in taxes in America despite billions in profits each year.

Towards the end of the 1990s, some key laws concerning banking and finance were changed and it set the stage for the worldwide economic problems in the first decade of this century.

Today the ultra-wealthy and their corporations are just parasites on America and the world. They contribute far less than they take. They have destroyed the American economy and they have destroyed many economies of many other nations, including many in Europe.

The ultra-wealthy and their corporations that are too powerful and that are referred to in English as "too big to fail" took control of

America's government and used their wealth and power to put an end to government regulation and oversight into corporate business that they consider "government interference" with their private business. They manipulated our banking laws, overinflated real estate prices and caused the real estate bubble. Their banks gave easy loans with deceptive contract terms that caused the real estate problem and the Wall Street problem and the financial crisis that almost crashed the world's economy in 2008.

In the American capitalist system, corporations believe that when they make profits they should be allowed to keep them, but if they lose money, that government taxes - taxes that are collected from working people - should pay for their losses and bail them out. And they have so much power from their wealth that they get away with this and the American people can do little to change it.

Between this attitude and actions by corporations and the corporate control of the U.S. government, along with the debt levels of Americans - many that no longer have jobs, and many more who have lost hope of finding jobs - and the ridiculously high military budget that keeps growing as our numerous wars continue while adding new conflicts in many places, it is no surprise that the United States is a nation in decline. It is also no surprise that Americans are jobless, in debt and losing hope in their future.

As an American that loves my country, I'm sorry to say that this is happening to it. Unfortunately it's true.

However, while all this is very bad for America and the American people, it is very good for China and the Chinese people.

China today is in a very similar position that America was in right after World War II, and later in this book I will explain how Chinese people can use American history to see where China is going and how China and Chinese people will prosper greatly from knowing and using America's 20th century history to China's advantage.

American history could also be used as a lesson in caution to avoid going beyond productive consumerism that built our great national wealth and into the destructive consumerism and business-dominated culture that caused the decline, and possible end, of my great nation.

*

Between the past and present and as we go into the future, there are other ideas and factors to consider.

Here are a few of them:

Energy

From the start of the Industrial Revolution and in the history of the 19th and 20th centuries, energy, especially oil, becomes a more important factor in the world. Energy and how it is used has resulted in a higher standard of living for many people in many nations and has also become an industry whose products earn extremely high profit margins.

With the advent of armored vehicles such as tanks in World War I, and the military dependence on aircraft, tanks and supply trucks in World War II, energy, especially oil, became one of the biggest factors in winning wars in the 20th century.

Germany depended heavily on its tanks and planes and when Hitler's military machine was slowly squeezed dry of oil it became apparent that the Allies would win the war. Japan too was cut off from oil by the United States prior to the U.S. entering the war and that directly led to Japan deciding to attack Pearl Harbor, make America a declared enemy and hopefully win its fight for oil. Fortunately for China and the United States that didn't happen. (Although we are all friends today, this is also a great example of how the U.S and China can work closely together to our mutual benefit. I hope we remember this if the time comes for disagreements between our two nations.)

In the early to mid-20th-century America had all the oil it needed. Our states of Texas, on Mexico's border, and Oklahoma had many productive oil wells. In America after World War II we had few energy problems. Abundant energy was one of the factors that contributed to the rise of consumer demand for many different types of products. And even through our rising standard of living during the 1950s America had few, if any, energy problems.

In the second half of the 20th century our consumer society was kicked into overdrive and Americans started buying many more products that reflected a higher standard of living in our culture. New technology and new inventions pushed this level of consumption higher and higher.

In the 1950s having a television became very important to American families. In the 1960s having one TV wasn't so special anymore, but having two TVs gave a family a higher status than other families. And color televisions, of course, when they became available also made people that owned them feel superior to those that only had black and white TVs. When remote controls were invented, everyone needed a television with a remote control - no one was happy if they had to get up and change the channel anymore.

In America, almost all middle class homes or apartments have washers and dryers, dish washers, ovens and garbage disposals.

The reason I mention these appliances in particular is because Americans love their kitchens and their comfort. They love to bake cakes and pies in ovens. They like to put dirty dishes in the dish washer and let the machine do the work while they watch TV, or today, as they surf the Internet. They hate doing laundry, but they like the fact that they can wash clothes and dry them quickly and get it over with. When I was a child I remember my mother hanging the clothes on the line outside to dry. Living on the second floor, she also had a line connected across our driveway to the building next door with the line looped around a pulley at each end - wheels with grooves - so she could attach the clothes to the line at the window and push them out into the breeze without having to go downstairs and outside.

Few lines like that exist today.

But in China, everyone has poles on their balconies to hang clothes or clothes racks outside where their clothes dry after washing.

Part of the reason for this today is because China is a very large country with many, many people. That's why energy is so much more important in China.

China is a wealthy country with abundant resources, but with so many people it is still difficult to keep up with the demand for energy. It would be even more difficult if most Chinese people had more appliances that use electricity.

To solve this problem, technology is helping, and China is moving in the right direction.

The world is developing and using more and more alternative sources of energy. Solar power, wind power and flowing water power are all being adapted more and more for use in consumer products. Recently, a floating wind turbine that could be moved and anchored off any coastline was tested off the coast of Portugal. If it isn't already in commercial production, it will be soon.

Today it is not practical for Chinese homes to have clothes dryers, but once consumer items such as solar-powered clothes dryers become typical and affordable, many Chinese people will buy them, and hanging clothes outside to dry will become a thing of the past. Demand for other household products powered by alternative sources of energy such as solar or wind will drive entrepreneurs to develop and market a wide range of household products to Chinese consumers. (As well as exporting these products to consumers around the world that are looking to cut costs.)

With less worries about energy and the high costs of energy such as electricity,

Chinese people will have the ability to choose to put ovens in their kitchen instead of just having a cook top as most kitchens have today. And Chinese people will have new foods available to them in their homes that they now have to go buy at restaurants or bakeries.

The cultural conversion to using dishwashers might take a little longer. Dishwashers took a while to become popular in America too because many people, especially housewives in the 1950s and 1960s, didn't want to appear lazy. Why have a machine do something that we can so easily do ourselves?

However, as people transition from poor or from lower-income working class people into the middle class they tend to indulge themselves more and buy products that they may not need, but that make their lives more comfortable - and that they can also compare to their friends and neighbors. (In English it is called "keeping up with the Joneses", "Jones" being a common family name in America, and its meaning is, the more you have that your neighbors don't, makes you more special than them.)

I believe, though, that with time and almost unlimited lower-cost energy, many Chinese people will start to use products like dishwashers that are more convenient and that make their lives more comfortable.

Garbage disposals are a different matter.

A garbage disposal is a machine that grinds leftover food items and washes them down the sink. It is located under the sink and attached to the drain of the sink. Water lubricates the food so the grinder works more easily and the leftover uneaten food is taken away with the same waste water as the water in your sinks today.

In America it is a convenience, but it's also a health issue.

When people leave uneaten food, or waste products from food we don't eat, like bones for example, animals will go through the trash and eat whatever they can find. This is what significantly increases the population of mice and rats. And mice and rats carry diseases that infect other animals, especially domestic animals like cats and dogs. The diseases also infect human beings either from exposure or contact, or contact with their cats and dogs that get the disease from the outside and bring it into the home.

In America we still have mice, rats and disease, but we have lowered the rates of diseases that are caught from mice and rats because there is little or no food left in the trash for them to eat.

I believe once this starts to happen in homes in China and Chinese homes have garbage disposals in their kitchen sinks, it will greatly increase the cleanliness and sanitation of Chinese cities and contribute to better health standards by reducing the mice and rat population.

And this can and will be achieved by the development and use of alternative energy as our planet moves away from using our dwindling supplies of oil.

Make no mistake about this: The world is running out of oil.

The problem is that Western oil companies will not allow new energy technology to compete with them and replace oil, until *every drop* of oil is *sold*. And once that is achieved they'll unveil new technology that they are already developing or already have but refuse to release to the people.

General Motors had a great fully electric car at the end of the 1990s that was tested, perfected and marketed in limited numbers. But as soon as the demand for them rose rapidly in America, GM was pressured by Western oil companies to stop it.

Despite favorable comments from everyone that had the cars and the growing market of consumers that were ready to buy electric cars and replace gas engines, the high cost of gas, the pollution from cars and the world conflicts due to oil, GM shut the program down. To do this, GM lied and claimed that there were flaws in the new technology and that the cars were not ready for consumers to buy.

(If you want to know the full story, look for the documentary movie, *Who Killed the Electric Car?*, it explains it all.)

If you want further proof that the world is running out of oil, despite oil company claims that everything is fine, just look at the oil industry itself.

The oil tankers are aging and should be replaced. Under normal circumstances, an industry like this that depended on tankers to ship its product to customers, would order new tankers. However, tankers are not only expensive but they take time to build. And oil companies know that by the time the new tankers are built, there won't be any oil to ship. So, they are saving the expense and continuing to use their old broken-down oil tankers.

**

Alternative energy development today has an interesting history that Chinese people should be aware of.

In the 1980s America was the leader in solar energy research.

Unfortunately, the U.S. government has been controlled by the ultra-wealthy and their corporations for many years now. And in the 1980s, Ronald Reagan, the U.S. president at the time, did the bidding of the very large and powerful Oil Industry and took all government research money away from the companies in America that were doing highly advanced solar energy research. The companies went out of business. Sometime after that and through the 1990s the center of solar power research moved to companies in Germany.

Remember, Germany not only has the largest economy in Europe but its economy was helped along after World War II by the Allies, and particularly America, that wanted to help it rebuild after it was virtually destroyed by war. (The same holds for Japan, which is why Japan became a large manufacturing nation and exported many products in the 1970s and 1980s.)

I don't know when it occurred, but sometime between the end of the 1990s and the first decade of the 21st century, China became the leader in the world in solar power research.

I believe this is very smart on China's part. I believe this will help speed China's development as an influential nation and world leader. I believe with the use of more solar power and other alternative forms of energy like wind power and wave or water power, China can solve its energy problems completely and independently provide energy for all Chinese people.

And this will make energy-powered consumer products more desirable and entirely possible for all Chinese people that want them.

It could also take China out of the numerous world conflicts over energy, such as the wars in the Middle East and disagreements about oil rich areas that other nations continue to argue about and fight over.

As I travel the highways in the area of China where I'm located I see many rooftops with solar water heaters. I wish I could say the same for America.

China also has high speed rail that America does not have. This is another indication that America is declining and China is rising.

In addition, many streetlights are solar powered.

There is also new technology that was used at the 2012 Olympics in London. It is a new type of sidewalk with tiles of the walkway designed to turn the kinetic energy from people stepping on them into electricity.

With the number of people walking city streets in every major city in the world, it would be crazy for world governments not to start putting this technology to use. This technology would be perfect for a country like China, with so many people available to create electricity from doing nothing more than what they are already doing - walking.

From what I've seen about how China operates, I'm betting that it will not be long before we see this technology used on China's sidewalks and the power generated by more than a billion people could greatly reduce China's need to buy foreign oil while greatly increasing China's energy and energy reserves.

New technology in wind turbines can (and will) also greatly aid in China's energy demands.

With the energy problem solved, and with new, abundant and low-cost energy for China's large population, nothing can stand in the way of China becoming the world leader of the 21st century.

China's Roadblocks to the Future

Keep in mind that nothing is perfect. And even though China is an emerging world leader it still has some international roadblocks to overcome.

I keep telling my Chinese friends that one of the biggest problems manufacturing in China has is quality control.

Virtually every product sold in the world is made in China today - except, of course, for bombs, bullets, cigarettes and hard liquor which America makes and sells in abundance.

Because everything is made in China, whenever anything is wrong with a product, or consumers complain that the quality is substandard, every American company is afforded the advantage of blaming it on the fact that the product is made in China.

It's no secret that I do not like Donald Trump and believe he is a reprehensible person, but he is a perfect example of America's anti-China attitude. This is a man who has an estimated worth of $94 billion but was able to declare bankruptcy four times under American laws that favor the wealthy and their corporations at the expense of our nation and people. And because he has so much money, his name is a brand name and he has a popular TV show where he selects other reprobates to learn from him and follow in his footsteps. He is arrogant, for no reason other than having money and making more money, and is constantly in the public eye in America. And since he is in the public eye, he never hesitates or misses an opportunity to blame many of America's problems on China.

Making negative comments about China however, doesn't stop him from having some of his brand name Donald Trump designer ties made in China for the lowest cost possible so that he can make the highest profits possible on sales in America. After all, he loves America and blames China for many things, but he wouldn't want to give jobs to Americans if it means paying them more than Chinese workers.

So let me tell you the truth of what's really happening.

Corporate demands to make products at the lowest possible cost have forced companies to use lower quality raw materials, lowest cost labor and/or pressures factories to do anything else that will cut costs. Because of these demands, quality control suffers. But American companies don't care because they can, and do, blame it on China and the Chinese factories that make everything any time there is a consumer complaint.

The dirty secret is that if American factories were still making any products, the same thing would be happening in America because those same cost-cutting factors would be hindering production and quality control there too.

But keep in mind that this is a factor today when foreign people or foreign countries take into account that the products they are using are made in China. It directly relates to China's reputation and the reputation of Chinese factories and Chinese workers.

**

Another issue between China and the West involves international laws. In America and between nations there are many laws concerning property rights. These laws protect intellectual property and inventions and have different areas such as copyrights, trademarks and patents.

Many Western nations and corporations are angry with China and Chinese businesses and factories for infringing on these property rights. Many Chinese companies have no problems taking a product and copying it to sell as their own. This is part of the reason that Western nations and companies are afraid to bring new ideas and new technology to China.

I'm not attempting to tell China or Chinese companies how to do business, but I am saying that this is an issue that needs the attention of Chinese businesses and factories. While I think this is an important international issue today, I think this problem will work itself out in China's immediate future if what I predict about China is correct.

Today China, Chinese businesses and Chinese manufacturers have no reason to care what foreigners think and international law has little effect on China. In China's future however, the issue of infringing on someone's copyright, trademark or patent will be less about those ideas or inventions of foreigners and more about those things that belong to other Chinese people. In other words, when the disputes become internal to China, Chinese people and Chinese companies, the legal system of China will have to respond and intervene in order to settle the dispute.

For the same reason, as Chinese factories make products for Chinese consumers, the quality control issue will be solved also. Chinese consumers will demand higher quality products and the factories that make those products will succeed in the large Chinese market of 1.4 billion consumers. The companies that fail to make high-quality products will simply go out of business.

The Future

All inventions and technology, from primitive tools and weapons to the iPad and beyond, all came about to fill a need that people had to survive or make life easier or be entertained or that just made them happy somehow.

The modern world went from the Industrial Revolution in the 1870s, through World War II to the Space Age that started when the Soviet Union launched a satellite in 1957. With the invention of computers, the world was pushed into a new age today. There are many names in English for this new period of history. It can be called the Age of

Technology, the Technological Age, the Computer Age or the Digital Age.

Regardless of what it is called, advanced technology is not only here to stay, but it develops and advances rapidly.

I bought a new laptop computer in 2001 that was on sale for half price because it was already obsolete. The new model, available in the store right next to the one I purchased, was already twice as fast and had more memory. This means that the technology developed so fast that there were still products in stores on the shelves by the time new products were designed, developed, manufactured, shipped and available for purchase, making the products already on the shelf old and almost outdated.

At least the advantage to consumers is that we can get relatively new products at bargain prices.

I tell Chinese business people over and over again the importance of keeping up with current trends, current technology and current research of coming technology.

Many new ideas and some consumer products start trends that take companies in directions that feed the desires of the buying public. If the trends do not die out too soon, many other companies try to take advantage of the trend by manufacturing their own products in the hope to gain some market share of whatever products are most popular at that time.

Remember, if the trend continues, there is a point where it is no longer a trend and it becomes a habit. There is no specific point in time or exact circumstances or reasons, but many ideas or inventions that lead to trends in consumer purchases, if popular enough, lead to buying habits. These are the creative ideas and products that become very popular, very profitable and that have built fortunes for companies and their owners.

In order to take advantage of the growing market for new ideas, good business leaders need to have a forward-thinking vision. Creative ideas and new technology of the kinds that feed consumer trends make some people, like (the now deceased) Steve Jobs of Apple, Bill Gates of Microsoft, and Jeff Bezos of Amazon, very rich.

Keep in mind that, in fact, there are two separate strategies here. One is that good business people almost have to be able to predict the future.

This is true. This is also not as hard as it sounds - especially for someone with knowledge of many different subjects, a good basis in creative thinking and the right information. As a matter of fact, constant research and information on what's going on in our crazy world along with what new research is being done in science, technology, agriculture, medicine and many other fields is essential.

With the right information good business people *can* predict the future.

The second idea is that good business people that have a forward-thinking vision and creativity not only have a good chance of predicting the future, but these are the visionary business leaders that can create their own future.

They do this by creating innovative products that start trends, and driving the demand for those products until the trends for their products becomes a habit for many consumers.

They also look at trends taking place already and use their creativity and forward-thinking vision to add to those trends and design something innovative, new and more exciting than what is taking place in the current trend.

Remember, no one can actually predict the future. However, if someone reads enough about history, culture, science, technology, psychology and human nature and gets an idea of what people desire or dream about, it is much easier to predict where the future will go and how people might react to new ideas, inventions or products. It is also easier to create the future by the vision of how people's needs can be met by new and more creative products.

It's no secret that I'm a big fan of Starbucks. (Although it surprises me that one of their most popular drinks in America, white-chocolate mocha, for some unknown reason is not offered on the menu in Asia. And they don't reply to customer emails.) Regardless, good business leaders can use Starbucks as an example of how to develop a company, how to develop a brand name and how to not only cater to consumer demands, but also how to drive those consumer demands while steering customers in the direction of their own products.

Many people in America were shocked at the high prices of coffee at Starbucks when it first started to become a nationally prominent brand. However, not only is their coffee higher quality and better tasting than average coffee products on the market or in other cafes, but the atmosphere they created in their shops contributed to the enjoyment that coffee drinkers and people that like to relax in cafes experienced.

So, while their products were priced higher, consumers were willing to pay higher prices.

In addition, the leadership team at Starbucks monitors consumer trends and buying habits and tries to respond to what they see. For example, the market of coffee made by people at home started to move to a preference to make one cup at a time.

In American culture, families would brew a pot of coffee in the morning to have with breakfast. For some people all they had was coffee. But making a pot of coffee and drinking only a cup or two is wasteful. In addition, rising coffee prices made consumers rethink their habit of wasting coffee and throwing away what they did not drink. Coffee drinkers also prefer *fresh-brewed* coffee, rather than coffee that has been sitting in a pot for a long time.

The solution was to make one cup at a time.

When one coffee company designed and produced a machine to do that, people bought it. The "one-cup" market soon expanded to an $8 billion a year segment of the coffee and one-cup-brewing machine market.

Starbucks saw this and struck a deal to make "one-cup" packets of its superior coffee for use in the widely selling one-cup coffee machines. And a year later, Starbucks announced that it decided to manufacture and market its own one-cup brewing machine.

Payment methods using new technology through cell phone applications to make paying for products easier and quicker was also introduced by Starbucks as soon as the technology became available.

There are other factors related to the way Starbucks conducts business and how it stays at the leading edge of the future as well, and that's why I always encourage prospective business leaders to read about the history of Starbucks, its development, its corporate image, its marketing strategies and its vision of how it grew to an internationally recognized brand that people literally go out of their way to purchase, even at higher prices, rather than settle for drinking average coffee that is readily available.

I'm also a big a fan of Amazon, and it is another company worth studying as an example of visionary leadership in the consumer market.

Jeff Bezos knew that online shopping would only grow faster and become a much larger part of the consumer market worldwide and he was smart enough to take advantage of that.

His brilliant decision to sell books online contributed to billions of dollars in the success of Amazon.

While that may sound simple on its face value, Bezos made some brilliant visionary decisions that made Amazon the powerful company that it is today and that made Bezos one of the wealthiest people in the world.

Bezos realized that there were many bookstores in the world. In America there were really two very large companies competing against each other. He also realized that while there were many books and many publishing companies, bookstores were limited in their size and inventory.

The Internet, however, has no such limits.

By listing virtually all titles available from virtually all book publishers, consumers could save time and effort as well as travel and transportation costs to bookstores in search of any book they were looking for. They could simply order them online from Amazon and the shipping fee would be far lower than the cost of time and transportation to find the books that they wanted.

This idea made Amazon a giant in retail sales.

However, Bezos didn't stop there. He knew that in the digital age people could access news and other information online and download files directly to their computers.

He envisioned having books available online to download so that consumers could use their computers or a new device such as an e-reader and eliminate the need for printed books.

This would also save the cost of printing and the additional cost of shipping the books to customers.

With the invention of Amazon's Kindle e-reader and other e-readers in this new very competitive market, and within a few short years, Amazon's digital book sales started to beat its online print book sales. And profits from both categories increased rapidly.

Keep in mind that during this time new technology continued to be developed. And one of these new types of technology was what's called "print on demand".

In the publishing world, companies that printed and sold an author's book had to print thousands of copies and distribute them to bookstores everywhere. If all those printed copies didn't sell, they sat on bookshelves taking up space. Eventually they are sold at deep discounts just to get rid of them.

With better and faster digital files, new computerized machines were developed that could take any formatted book file and by entering information into the computer the new printer could manufacture a book of any size, with any size print and any type of binding. Any cover could be manufactured immediately also, from expensive leather hardcovers to less expensive paper covers or glossy photo-quality covers.

One suggestion made to Bezos was that Amazon start its own bookstore. This bookstore would be an entirely new business model.

This bookstore would be a bookstore and café where only samples of books would be available to see and touch. The samples could be any book, but would allow customers to see the pages, the print, and binding, so they could decide what format of book they preferred.

Descriptions of all books available would be in their online catalog at the store.

Once a customer decided to purchase a book, they could wait with a cup of coffee or a snack while large printing machines in the back room of the store "made" their book. And in under an hour they could leave the store with the book they came in to buy.

All books would be available and they would never be told that the store didn't have a copy of the book they were looking for.

This gave Bezos some options of which direction to go in and where to invest his and the company's money.

Under the visionary leadership of Bezos, however, he knew the bleak future of retail stores and the rise of online shopping and decided against the idea of brick and mortar retail stores, complete with all their unnecessary expenses that are avoided in Internet commerce. Instead he focused on e-books and his Kindle e-reader.

This turned out to be a brilliant business decision and game-changing strategy.

Amazon is by far the largest online store today and made about $48 billion in revenue in 2011. About half of its revenue comes from sales of movies, music, TV shows, print books and ebooks. And while books in general outsell most other Amazon products, e-books are a large portion of that fifty-percent.

As a side note, the success of Amazon has been taking some advertising revenue away from another large international company - Google.

Google is the most well-known search engine online in the West. Google makes much of its income from advertising. However, rather than do a search on Google for products, consumers now are going directly to Amazon and searching Amazon's site for products and purchasing them there once they find what they are looking for.

This opens up all new possibilities for the future and competition of Internet businesses.

*

When one considers the future there are many different areas to take into account.

Let's look at the future in terms of one thing only - getting products to market.

Shipping.

America moved manufacturing to China because low labor costs resulted in very high profits for Western companies despite the fact that all products needed to be loaded into containers, placed on ships and sent across the ocean to foreign ports.

With the world running out of oil today, the global conflicts caused by the worldwide need for oil and the rising costs of oil, shipping is more and more expensive each month.

Eventually this can only lead to a "tipping point" when the savings on labor are not as important as the higher costs of shipping products from factories in China to stores in America.

Put that together with the powerful business interests in America that have been systematically attacking organized labor and breaking unions making the bargaining power of workers much weaker today than we've ever had in America.

Strong unions and the power of organized labor contributed to America's prosperity. And they helped create the middle class that pays virtually all the taxes today. Workers are more productive when they are happy and they feel they are receiving wages that they deserve. They also feel respected by their employers.

American car company founder Henry Ford, who introduced the idea of the assembly line concept of mass production to American car manufacturing, also believed that workers should be paid enough to afford their own products. He believed this would lead to good morale, increased productivity and, ultimately, prosperity for the company.

In America today, (and the world), international corporations have turned that idea around.

American corporations are trying to take advantage of the many unemployed American workers who today are desperate for work. However, since the cost of living is higher in America and even staple foods are expensive, many out-of-work Americans are still not willing to work for the same wages Chinese people get paid. American corporations are trying very hard, however, to force Americans to accept lower and lower wages.

If these companies, for example, achieved this tomorrow, they would close factories in China immediately and save money on labor *and* shipping.

Fortunately for China and Chinese workers, this isn't likely. At least not yet.

The unavoidable fact is, however, that when the cost of shipping outweighs the cost of labor, the companies will not hesitate to close factories in China and move back to America where even if they pay higher wages they continue to make profits on lower shipping costs.

Oil, of course, is a factor, but keep in mind that as we talk about the future, anything is possible.

Before products were shipped across the oceans in cargo ships, or container ships, fueled by oil, they were powered by steam. And before steam, ships used sails. Today, due to the world situation with oil, there are companies designing and building modern sailing ships with automatic sails controlled by a computer for maximum efficiency. The new designs also have small engines to power the ship when needed, but most of the time they will use sails, with computers calculating the right angles of the sails to catch every bit of wind, so they can save energy and help the environment as they ship products to foreign markets.

Today there is also high speed rail. Trains go faster and faster. And China is a leader in the world already in high speed rail taking Chinese passengers from city to city in such a large country.

Technology is available today, however, that is even better than high speed rail.

There is new technology of trains running in vacuum tubes and powered by magnets that if built across the ocean can take people from America to China in two hours.

If this technology is adapted for shipping products, it is an international commerce game changer. Cargo ships and even energy efficient sailing ships will all be obsolete. On land, traditional railroads and even trucks could be easily replaced by this technology too.

*

Sometimes when considering the future we have to completely abandon everything we know and accept about the present. This is true of the future of retail stores.

There is something happening in stores around the world today that should be terrifying to store owners. It's called *showrooming*, and it will continue until it ends traditional commerce as we know it today.

Brick and mortar stores cannot compete with online shopping. This is just a fact that nothing can be done to change.

Stores are buildings that have to be owned or rented. Store owners need furniture, products on display, lights, air conditioning, cash registers, salespeople, possibly other employees and some type of management. (Although in today's business climate managers get paid more and more for doing less and less, while workers contribute to most of what a company profits from but get paid the least.)

Due to these operating expenses, or what in English is called *overhead*, prices for products in stores cannot be nearly as low as they are online.

This is why store owners worldwide are starting to see many people come in to their stores looking for products that they want or that they saw somewhere in advertising. And rather than buy the item in the store, they are taking a photo with the camera in the cell phones that everyone carries today. Many also write down the brand and model number. Then they simply leave the store without making a purchase, go home, get online and buy the product at a much lower price.

As this continues to happen more and more, many stores will go out of business. Stores cannot survive by being physical showrooms for companies that sell the same products online.

If this trend continues, and I believe it will, there is the possibility that, in time, our entire shopping experience as we know it today will change completely.

I don't know how many years this will take if something else doesn't come about to change my prediction, and I know I am jumping a little ahead in time, but eventually we may make all our purchases online and the only stores left to physically shop in will be supermarkets with fresh produce such as fruits and vegetables, restaurants and specialty stores or convenience stores that carry products that we cannot do without.

We can shop for almost anything online today, but delivery takes time. There are some products, like toothpaste or baby's diapers or women's products that if people run out of them at home, they cannot wait for a delivery, they must buy them right away.

This will cause a rise in neighborhood convenience stores that carry many of these items. Most convenience stores today have higher prices for many items found in supermarkets, but consumers are willing to pay those prices for the *convenience* of not having to go to a shopping center or of having to find a large supermarket. So, consumers will easily accept higher prices at convenience stores.

However, they will only buy items there if they run out of products that they usually buy in their weekly or monthly online shopping.

Many convenience stores may even offer online shopping for quick local neighborhood delivery.

The good news of this possible future increase in online shopping is that it will create more opportunities for shipping and delivery companies like FedEx, DHL, UPS and SF. Or *your* delivery company if you want to get into a business with a solid and growing future.

Specialty stores will still exist, but they may operate differently.

Car dealerships is a good example of this concept.

If people continue to buy cars, they will want to see, touch and probably test drive a car before buying it. This is not a product that someone would buy online without at least first looking at the real thing. Car dealers will still have brick and mortar locations where potential customers can do this. But the dealers will probably not have an inventory of cars available for purchase. They will stock display cars and test-drive cars only and the dealer will probably take an order from the customer and have the car manufactured on demand.

Manufacturing products that sit around and wait for consumers to purchase them is very inefficient, but it's how we do business today. I believe that a change in attitude between producers and consumers, and with the help of advanced technology, given time, this will change also. Most products will be made on demand, in small amounts, rather than in the thousands or hundreds of thousands.

In some cases this might cause technology to be used less in manufacturing in favor of workers that can make products in required quantities while controlling quality. In other words, it would be more advantageous for workers to make products rather than large commercial robotics that will not be manufacturing the large quantities they were designed for today.

For a product like cars, showrooms will still exist where people can go and physically see the car, but the dealers will probably also have websites where customers can shop once they decide to buy. This will cause competition between car companies online also. It will also change the business model of buying cars, in which companies would have to offer much lower prices or discounts in order to sell their products.

Keep in mind that the owner of a car dealership with a showroom will also have to compete with an owner of an online car dealership who may not have a showroom, where customers can purchase the cars for less because the owner has no showroom and therefore less overhead.

In a futuristic online car dealership, for example, the dealership owner could have a few of his cars driving around town with website advertising printed on all sides. He could also park on streets with many restaurants as a form of display to advertise his product. He could also offer test-drives anywhere he may be. And you will see as you keep reading that there will be many more restaurants for this type of car dealer to park near.

People will be able to see and touch the car and then shop for it online if they choose to do so.

*

Whenever I discuss all these futuristic ideas, I have many friends that say that customers will always want to touch products and that's why there will always be stores.

I disagree.

As we know things today and with today's technology, yes. But, we're talking about tomorrow. When the automobile was invented there were many people that said we would always use horses for transportation and that this crazy new invention would not replace horses. Well, people still ride horses today, but few of them ride their horses to work or to the supermarket.

With today's technology we still need to go to stores to try on clothes or shoes or just to touch and feel a product that we are afraid to purchase online.

However, this is something else that will greatly improve with advanced technology.

And with improved technology the attitude of consumers will change.

When Internet shopping started many people were afraid to use their credit card information online - and the truth is that there are thieves that steal information and identities - but advanced technology made the security much better and shopping online is routine today for many people.

Today, shoppers can purchase clothing online in various standard sizes such as small, medium and large.

Wealthy people can go to stores or tailors and have clothes custom made.

The manufacturing process needs to catch up a little with technology, but it is possible today for consumers to enter specific data of their clothing sizes and get the right size clothes from any online store that offers this option. There probably aren't many right now that offer anything other than standard sizes, but there will be more of these stores once consumers demand clothing that fits them better than the one-size-fits-all concept.

And the technology, along with Internet sales, will make it affordable for all.

As we advance into the future and with an attitude change and the aid of technology it will be easier to move from a one-size-fits-all mentality to a market where almost anyone, regardless of wealth, can get custom fit clothing.

With better manufacturing technology and a new attitude of selling and buying online, this will happen eventually. I'm not saying it might happen, I'm saying it will happen.

In the near future we will also shop using hologram technology. A consumer can enter his or her body measurements into a computer program that will create a holographic image that they can then use to *try on* clothing that they like and may want to buy. Women will especially be drawn to this because they can look at themselves from any angle and see how the clothes look on them before they make the purchase.

And all this will be done in the convenience of your own home while sitting at the computer sipping your favorite drink. No more wasted time and energy going from store to store to find what you are looking for.

Technology is changing our societies, as it always does, and it will continue.

The one type of brick and mortar business that will survive in the future will be restaurants.

People are social beings. We love to get together with friends and family. We also love to eat. We especially love to get together with friends and family to eat!

We especially love to eat in restaurants where we don't have to cook, dirty up the kitchen or spend time cleaning the kitchen or washing dishes after eating.

Restaurants, as well as any business that depends on social gatherings, like live theater or concerts or nightclubs will continue to thrive in our future.

Supermarkets will still exist too. Some, however, might offer online shopping and delivery as an option also. Most people, I believe, will continue to shop for fresh food items such as fruits and vegetables or fish, meat and eggs and similar items that they can select for themselves.

In any event, aside from supermarket grocery shopping, socializing will be the biggest reason for people to leave their homes and go out in town, and going to restaurants will play a large part in that.

This will change the restaurant industry also. There will be much more competition for diners. Customers will have an abundance of choices.

In today's business climate, people that open restaurants are very careful about what type of restaurants they open and where. For example, it's stupid to open an Indian restaurant right next to another Indian restaurant. The same idea holds with pizza or Thai food or any other type of restaurant.

Smart business owners today may locate their restaurant in the same neighborhood or on the same street as another of its kind, but far enough away that it doesn't have to compete with that similar restaurant. But this may change in the future.

Since there won't be clothing stores or shoe stores or toy stores as a buffer between restaurants like there are today, many more restaurants will be located next door to each other and it is inevitable that many similar restaurants will be in close proximity to each other.

This will make restaurants much more competitive.

One thing restaurants will start doing is selling window space to products like clothing or other items such as computers or cell phones that can be displayed in the window for restaurant customers to look at while waiting for a table or just passing by. Many restaurants are usually very busy and it is not uncommon to have to wait until other people are finished eating before a table is available. And people have to do something while they are waiting.

Advertising for products in the restaurant windows is a strategy that can and will be mutually beneficial for the restaurant and Internet companies selling products.

The restaurant can work with the online company and offer discounts on the company's products when given a discount code from the restaurant. And in turn the Internet company can give a discount code for food and beverages at the restaurant to any customer that purchases products from ads displayed in the restaurant window.

This will open up new and much more creative avenues for marketing and advertising where the few businesses that will survive the future economy of online shopping can work closely with the online companies so that they both benefit from consumer purchases.

In reality, other than supermarkets for fresh food, showrooms for products like cars, neighborhood convenience stores and restaurants, there will be little need for stores that sell any other products. Everything will be available online.

Keep in mind that I'm only offering ideas of the possibilities in our near future. I say near future because great new ideas are being turned into great new inventions every day at this point in time and something new and brilliant could change everything we know.

In general, technology can be a great thing and advance humanity for the better. Sometimes, however, it can be destructive.

Regardless of whether inventions are good or bad, new technology will be invented, and "good" or "bad" depends on how we use that new technology. I can only hope that any new technology created will heal our ailing environment, bring all people together in harmony and world peace and solve our many problems of disease, poverty, starvation and homelessness.

I guess that remains to be seen.

China's Future

In 2001, Gordon Chang, a well-respected American lawyer who appears regularly on American news and opinion shows, wrote a book called *The Coming Collapse of China*, claiming, for many reasons, that China's economy would collapse by 2006. He was obviously wrong. This is a great time for China in the history of the world and it's a great time to be Chinese.

American and international corporate greed put China and the Chinese people in a prosperous position, far ahead of the rest of the world. While other nations suffer from serious financial problems, China has abundance and wealth.

Despite the fact that they have destroyed the American economy, American corporations closed factories in America to come to China. Their greed and pursuit of low-cost labor far outweighed any other factor. They knew they were destroying the American economy and putting American labor out of work, which has caused the decline of our nation and has pushed middle class Americans into poverty, but they didn't care. They only saw over a billion Chinese people that were so desperate for work that they were willing to work for pay that in America is considered *slave wages*. That's an interesting English play on words because slaves usually don't get any wages.

What the corporations actually did was sacrifice long term profits and long term stability for very high short term profits. This is bad for America and the American workers, but ultimately it will be devastating to the corporations themselves.

All of this, however, is very good for China, the Chinese people and especially Chinese workers.

As a matter of fact, because American corporations closed factories in America and moved to China this is the main reason that China will be the world leader in the 21st century.

At the end of World War II, America was the world's factory. China is the world's factory today. And because China is the world's factory, it has been further enriched and fueled since the late 1980s by the wealth China accumulated from Western consumers. China today is wealthy, prosperous and debt free, while other nations are in severe decline and can't finance their own needs such as roads, bridges, electric grids or social programs for the poor or elderly.

The decline of Western nations along with the prosperity from Chinese manufactured exports is contributing to China's inevitable rise as a world power.

Since most people in the world are low-wage workers or poor, an increase in the number of jobs along with continuing raises in wages greatly increases the wealth of a nation. With an increase in jobs and wages there is also an increase in individual wealth. An increase in individual wealth also contributes to an increase in the size of the middle class of a nation. And an increasing middle class continues to feed the increased prosperity of a nation. And when people become wealthier and have more disposable income they like to buy products that make their lives easier. If every Chinese person could afford a car, how many of them would continue to walk or ride a bicycle to work?

When a nation rises in status in the world and becomes powerful, its people also experience a rise in their standard of living. A rise in standard of living usually involves people making more money, becoming wealthier and buying more products that make them comfortable and happy.

And again, these feed on each other and are mutually beneficial.

As a nation prospers from its production, growth and exports and the growth of its middle class workers, that nation's standard of living rises, in part, because the nation has enough wealth to build or upgrade its infrastructure. New roads, bridges, electric grids, sanitation, water purification, high speed rail and other areas of the national infrastructure benefit from this growth and wealth. In addition, social programs for the poor and elderly can be more generously funded.

Due to world events and China manufacturing, the people of China are lucky enough to have many jobs today. And in the coming years, more people that want jobs will be able to get them.

I grew up during the tail end of American prosperity. College was expensive and I had to earn money to pay for it. And because of the American prosperity at the time, I usually worked two to three part-time jobs for my entire time in college.

A time like that is fast approaching in China. Since jobs will be available, many people will choose to work two jobs and sacrifice some free time to earn more money. Eventually the money they earn will push them up into China's growing middle class.

Today there are roughly 200 million people in China that earn enough money to be considered Middle Class. One prediction by Western business analysts is that by 2025 China will have 520 million people in the middle class.

At this point in time I believe that figure may be low. I think China is developing rapidly and faster than Western business analysts are predicting. That means there will be even more middle class people in China than they expect there to be.

In 2011 China's wages rose by 12.4%. Wages are still not high enough, but it's a start. Last year China's economy surpassed Japan's and is now the second largest economy in the world. Some economists predict that China will surpass the U.S. and have the world's largest economy sometime between 2016 and 2020. Just as middle class incomes fueled American expansion for thirty years after World War II, China's large workforce and growing middle class will drive the rise of China as the world leader in this century.

Although it would not be good for international business or international relations, there could come a time when China could leave the West completely behind. Today, China doesn't need the West, the West needs China.

Since technology is making our world smaller and smaller each day, diplomacy between nations is and will continue to be important. However, it is a fact today that Western nations need China's manufacturing capability and in the very short term cannot do without it. That already makes China a more powerful nation on the world stage.

As I write this in 2012, manufacturing in China has declined slightly. The reason for this is obvious. Western nations have no money. They're broke. They were hit hard by the financial problems created by Wall Street, the large international banks and the large international corporations. Many European and American consumers have slowed their buying habits and are only purchasing essential products.

This trend will continue as people spend more of their savings, borrow more money to survive and try to exist either without jobs or dangerously under-employed.

Partly in response to this and partly due to the rise in the standard of living in China due to China's current export wealth, Chinese people are becoming consumers.

The consumer society of China is something that Western nations and companies have been dreaming about for years, like how young men dream of marrying beautiful movie stars.

Remember, companies love to sell products. If they can sell one, they try to sell two. If they sell two they try to sell four. And American companies can do math, unlike most American schoolchildren, and they know that there are only 300 million Americans. That means 300 million potential customers. But the market potential in China is 1.4 billion.

I, for example, would be very happy if only 1% of Chinese people bought a copy of this book. Despite a low cost and low profit margin, I would be very happy with 1% of sales.

As another example of the potential of the Chinese consumer market, I am publishing this book in both English and Chinese. I could just publish it in Chinese, but the fact is that today there are more people in China that speak and read English today than there are *people* in America. Yes, this is a fact today - over 300 million Chinese people speak English. (By contrast, I've heard of about two or three Americans, give or take one or two, that speak Chinese) (And although I'm joking about that, the number of Chinese-speaking Americans is very low. However, the smart ones, knowing that China is rising to world leadership today, are beginning to learn Chinese and are ensuring that their children learn it.)

As China develops faster and rises as a world leader it may continue to be difficult for Western companies to introduce their products to Chinese consumers. Part of the reason for this is that Western companies do not want to compromise on price and sell products for lower profits even if the volume of Chinese sales would be huge. But eventually there will be some imported products that Chinese consumers will want to buy.

However, what will drive Chinese economic prosperity and contribute greatly to the increase in the Chinese Middle Class will be Chinese companies producing products for Chinese consumers.

When 1.4 billion Chinese people start to become consumers along with earning higher wages in all the factories and companies making products for 1.4 billion Chinese consumers, there will be an economic boom that will shake the world.

Chinese factories will dramatically increase production and companies will even add space or open additional factories to accommodate the demand. In turn, even more Chinese people wanting jobs will find them. There will be many jobs available in all skill levels, from low wage manual labor jobs to high tech labor requiring advanced schooling and knowledge gained through college and direct experience.

The increased wages, along with the increasing number of jobs created by consumer demand, will, in itself, create more consumer demand for all types of products made in all types of factories.

Wages will increase, of course, due to the demand of factories for more and more workers to handle their increased production.

This is the way it will work: There will be two factories making the same product and trying to keep pace with the demand for that product by Chinese customers. The factory owner will realize that he or she will have an edge in the marketplace if production is increased or the skill level of workers is raised. This will lead to a slight increase in wages and attract more workers. Especially skilled and experienced workers.

Workers at the other factory will hear that workers doing the same job they are doing are being paid more money at the rival factory. This will cause some of them to quit and take their experience to the factory paying more money for their labor.

The factory losing workers will have no choice but to raise pay for its workers also.

And for a period of time, due to the demand for products and increased profits coming from sales of products that Chinese people want to buy, Chinese wages will continue to rise.

This process will feed on itself and cause the Chinese economy to expand greatly while causing a giant expansion in the Chinese Middle Class.

It will be prosperity for all. The companies will profit, the workers will profit and the country will profit. It will be mutually beneficial for all. It will mirror the American expansion and prosperity experienced after World War II.

The other problem that this will solve in China is quality control.

One of the biggest problems in China today is that Western companies demand products for the lowest costs possible. And the only way to accomplish this is to cut costs on materials, labor or production. This is a problem today because it is believed that many of the products coming from China are substandard.

I continuously warn my Chinese friends that what Western companies are doing is forcing Chinese manufacturers to make hard choices of cutting costs while trying to make the highest quality products possible. This is not easy, however. Sometimes it's impossible.

And when substandard products make it into the American consumer market and Americans complain about the products, who do you think the American companies blame? China, Chinese manufacturers and Chinese workers.

Under the developing economic rise of China, this problem will be solved very easily. The factories that make high quality products will survive during competition for Chinese customers and the factories making low quality products will go out of business.

*

This is the process that will continue for a period of twenty to thirty years and develop China's economy rapidly and create and expand a middle class that will be the envy of every nation, just as the American middle class was the envy of other nations in the 20th century. It will also make China wealthy beyond belief, giving it wealth and status far ahead of the declining Western nations and making it the world leader in the 21st century.

If China continues on this current path, this is what will most likely happen, barring anything unusual happening in the world or new game-changing technology that makes everything I predict wrong.

If this is indeed the path China takes, whatever happens after the next thirty or forty years or between the years from forty to seventy years or eighty years is anyone's guess. However, the next section includes some possible situations.

The Not-So Distant Future

If history continues on its current course and nothing major happens to change things, China should follow the path I've explained as it happened in America. Remember, I'm not attempting to predict anything, I'm just teaching a little history of how America became the world leader that it was in the 20th century and how that position is transferring to China in this century.

If nothing changes and this is indeed the path China follows, in America's footsteps, then it stands to reason that, advances in technology aside, China will also follow a similar path that America followed to the end of the 20th century and into the 21st century.

That means China would have about sixty years, more or less, of growth and prosperity before things begin to change as they changed in America.

After raising wages as high as they want to, Chinese companies will be looking for less costly ways to manufacture their products, while continuing to keep up with consumer demands.

Who knows what new technology will exist in fifty years? And new technology, especially if it comes sooner than later, could change everything I've said here.

One thing I continue to focus on, as a deep thinking person, is what companies will do if there are no customers for their products.

For example, the growing trend in using robotics in factories has me worried very much.

Currently, in our world today, people need jobs to make money and they need money to buy basic things like the most important of all, food. The list of essential things certainly includes food, housing, clothing and when needed, medical care.

It's no secret that when the economy is bad people cut down on non-essential things and only buy what they need.

With more and more factories using robotics, people are losing jobs. So far in China that hasn't been a major problem. However, workers in other countries are feeling the effects of this already.

It's true that productivity is much better with robotics and computers aiding in manufacturing any product.

The problem I cannot help thinking about, however, is that if people do not have jobs, they have no money and if they have no money, they not only can't buy essential things like food, but the last things they will consider buying are any other non-essential items.

In other words, companies can greatly increase productivity using robotics, but if robotics replaces all workers, then in the long run there are no customers for all those products that are so efficiently made by robotics.

How will people survive? How will they get food? What will people use to get or "buy" food?

We would possibly have to change our entire way of thinking. And when I say "we" I mean all human beings, not nations or governments.

I believe that some robotics can help us make products much more efficiently but if we continue to replace workers with robotics and we don't change our basic philosophies of how people survive in modern society, then it will be very, very bad for all people.

That belief as I just stated it is mostly philosophical.

As a question of business and commerce, the issue becomes more relevant and realistic. If robots make every product and there are much fewer workers, who will buy the products?

It seems simple, but companies are still replacing workers today with robotics in order to gain short term profits and most companies are not thinking about the long term.

Another big issue facing China today is competition with India.

When the new China emerges as the world leader and a consumer society, I don't think this will be a problem.

Some factories located in China might move to India to take advantage of lower cost labor as Chinese wages rise.

They will do this for the very same reasons American companies moved from America to China. India has many poor and desperate people that would be happy with any job at any level of pay.

However, products imported to China will have transportation costs and tariffs, or import taxes, and those will increase the costs of the products, raising the consumer prices of the products.

Therefore, it would be smarter for Chinese factories to stay in China.

The possibility exists, of course, that factories in India will be exporting products to all the nations that China is currently exporting to today. But as I keep saying, once Chinese consumers are buying Chinese-made products, China will not need any other country to buy any of its products. Export products would be a bonus on top of domestic sales.

If all goes as I've predicted, the distant future will be what Chinese people need to focus on.

As far as the distant future, it's much harder to predict.

What contributed to America's downfall was the leveling of wages in the 1970s. Workers' wages leveled off, but the cost of living increased. The costs of manufacturing products increased for companies, but they in turn increased prices.

American consumers were hit twice. With pay leveling off, in reality they made less money, while prices continued to increase.

At first it caused more housewives to go back to work because the family needed the income from both working parents. Families could no longer survive on just the father's income.

The trap of easy credit was laid by banks, however, to compensate for less wages and rising prices. And American workers took the bait. They borrowed money and went into debt.

Between the banks, Wall Street and corporations exercising too much power and taking over the American government, American workers and consumers suffered, went into debt and as of 2012 we not only have not recovered, but there is no recovery in sight.

I can only hope that the laws in China are different and that the Chinese people learn from America's mistakes and don't allow this to happen to the Chinese people.

As we move even further into the distant future, I think that if the same events happen in China that contributed to America's decline as a world leader, then China's only probable threat will come from Africa.

If this is a possibility - and I'm not saying it is a good possibility, it is too far in the future to predict - and if China's future follows as closely to the model of America's past that I'm using in this book, then businesses operating in China will stall Chinese wages, then begin moving factories to Africa, where there will possibly be many more desperate and poor people willing to work for wages that are much lower than future Chinese workers will be getting paid.

One thing is for sure - at my age today, I certainly won't be around at that time to see if I'm right or wrong.

But who knows? New technology could be invented in my lifetime that extends all of our lives by fifty or one-hundred years.

China and U.S. Cooperation

I would like to say a word about U.S. and China relations.

I believe the U.S. and China can remain great friends and continue to be great friends and partners in any future scenario. I believe our two cultures have much to offer each other.

However, in world history, any interaction between nations always comes down to two options - they will be friends or enemies.

If enemies, the destruction to both our nations and the world will be unimaginable.

If friends, the combination of our cultures and creativity can advance the world and humanity to realities not thought possible today.

For the sake of the world and our two countries, I hope we remain friends.

I can list possible points of conflict and problems that may occur between our nations, but this book isn't about any of that and it is not about politics. It's about business and China and China's future as a world leader and business leader in the world in this century.

So, I will leave this section with only the thought that I hope the U.S. and China remain friends and important allies in the future to the benefit of humanity and the world.

Conclusion

Part of the reason I wrote this book was to help my hard-working Chinese friends who I believe deserve prosperity. I would hope that their prosperity would go hand in hand with the prosperity of hard-working people worldwide.

Another reason for writing this is that my Chinese friends don't know American history very well. And by not knowing America's 20th century history, they can't realize how much power they actually have in the world. Chinese workers are prospering and wages are beginning to rise at a time when many nations are suffering from very high unemployment. The country is wealthy and on a solid financial foundation. The nation's infrastructure is expanding and being built using the newest technology. And the large population, rather than being a burden with so many people, is actually the biggest advantage of all.

One thing is certain, however, we live in interesting, exciting and with all probability, dangerous times. And at times is seems as if anything can happen.

If the world continues on its current path, I believe that everything I've said in this book will most likely happen.

However, keep in mind that this is a general statement. This history should play out in a similar way to how it happened in the United States, barring anything unusual in the world, such as a major world war that China may be involved in, or an environmental catastrophe in China, Asia or the world, an epidemic or global pandemic, a world economic meltdown that effects every nation or even something crazy like an alien invasion or an impact from an asteroid such as the one that is generally believed to kill the dinosaurs over 65 million years ago. I believe anything is possible.

But if the world goes on, as it is, and despite the variables or possibilities or changes due to future technology or any concept I discussed in this book, China will have the advantage of being in the right place at the right time in history.

Here is something to keep in mind: If some, or any, of my predictions come true and China becomes the world leader in this century, it can thank America's ultra-wealthy and the corporations they own for destroying the American economy, crushing organized labor, taking control of the U.S. government and ensuring that laws were written and passed to favor their class and their companies, despite the fact that they hurt our nation, our people and our economy (as well as the environment and other nations and people). They, America's ultra-wealthy and their corporations, are the main reason for China's position and power in the world today and the reason that China is the "world's factory." They are the reason that China is prosperous today from exports, and they are the reason that China is rising rapidly as a developed nation and the world leader.

And they are the main reason for America's decline.

There is a fable in Western culture called The Scorpion and the Frog. It's about a scorpion that wants to cross a river, and since it can't swim, it asks a frog to take it across on the frog's back. The frog tells the scorpion that he doesn't want to carry him on his back because the scorpion will sting him and kill him. The scorpion claims that it would be stupid of him to do that because he would also die since he can't swim. So, the frog agrees to carry the scorpion across the river on its back. The frog swam and kicked hard to stay at the surface so the scorpion would be safe, above the water. And halfway across the frog felt a sharp sting in its back. The frog turned its head to see the scorpion pulling the stinger out of the frog's back as it felt its arms and legs start to go numb so it could no longer swim. The frog asked the scorpion why it did that, since both of them would drown now. And the scorpion said, "It's my nature."

The American corporations are like the scorpion and the frogs are the American people who were also, in good times, their workers and consumers. And in a twist to the original story, the corporations got wealthy beyond belief from American workers and the American working class and middle class consumers that bought all their products. And, as the true scorpions that they are, it is their nature to expand and continue to search for lower costs and higher profits, while killing the frogs that made them what they are today.

Walmart, a company, and the family that owns it, that I detest, is a perfect example of the destructive nature of these large global corporations. In every city where they've built their large department stores, they've coerced the governments to violate the very nature of capitalism by giving tax payer subsidies to finance their buildings, their roads and even their labor costs by helping underpaid employees fill out government assistance forms for tax-paid programs that help the needy. Except that these needy people are Walmart employees. In addition, the company, as well as the Walton family that owns it, avoids paying their fair share of taxes. And on top of that, because they pay Chinese workers insultingly low wages, they make extremely large profits. But that's still not good enough for them. They still want more.

In addition, in every city where they have opened a store, their buying power and ability to sell products at an unfairly low price, due to the subsidies it gets from our governments and the low cost products it gets from China, the local stores cannot compete and eventually they all go out of business.

In the long term they will be left without customers as more and more Americans stop buying products they don't really need and only concentrate on essential things like food, basic clothing and medicine.

Part of the Walmart strategy, however, is to not only operate globally, with no allegiance to any nation or people, but also to be the only store left. And once all competition is eliminated, it can charge any price for any product to the consumers that are left.

Luckily for China, that's not going to be a problem. China is on a different and independent path. The slowdown in manufacturing as I write this in 2012 and the loss of Western customers are a small bump in the road towards China's future.

So, with the loss of American consumers and many customers from other Western nations, China will go on its own path to future power and prosperity. Of all the nations currently in the world, China is the only one positioned to take the baton from America and run swiftly to its future, far ahead and unhindered by other competitors.

So, to my Chinese friends I say, continue doing what you are doing. Keep learning, keep thinking, keep improving yourself and keep looking to the future with a new and creative eye. You are in the right place at the right time in history, and as we say in English, *the world is your oyster*. Take the baton and run. No one stands in your way.

****

Appendix A:

Business Ideas: There are many stories and examples that can be taken from American history during its prosperous post-World-War II years and that can be easily adapted to Chinese culture. Chinese entrepreneurs only need to discover these and replicate them in China.

For example: There have been some very ambitious independent people in America that would go to a car dealer looking for a car. But instead of purchasing or leasing a car, they worked a deal with the owner that if they got five people to lease identical cars, the owner would give a discount on the five leased cars and give them a car for free. Dealership owners agreed, since this was a win-win situation for them - giving discounts is possible and giving one car for free after leasing five is still very profitable. It's like having an additional employee selling your product that you don't have to pay a salary or benefits to - and a free car is a very low sales commission. The motivated independent salesperson then goes to various professionals, such as doctors or lawyers and offers them a discount on a specific type of luxury car with many options. And he doesn't stop until he gets five that agree to the contract. The dealer leases five cars at once, for a small discount and the independent salesperson gets a car for free.

Many people also live in luxury in America without paying rent by becoming house sitters for wealthy people that either travel frequently or live in one of their houses and want their other house (or houses) to be maintained, cleaned each day and protected from burglars or squatters, from the appearance of being occupied every day.

In another case, I'm not sure when it happened or who started it, but some brilliant entrepreneur was smart enough to cross cultures between America and China and took full advantage of one situation: chicken feet.

As far as I know, no Americans eat chicken feet. In America if we buy whole chickens, they are packaged and sold without the feet or head. The poultry industry used to just throw the feet away. And as far as the heads, it may be a cultural difference in America, but most Americans don't like their food to look back at them. It frightens them.

So, I don't know where, when or how it happened, but someone, somewhere realized that Chinese people loved to eat chewy chicken feet. Therefore, rather than discard the feet, chicken feet are now one of the largest exported products from America to China.

In other words, chicken feet went from non-profit-generating trash in America to very profitable exports to China.

These are just a couple of examples of creative thinking in designing a business that might work for you.

The fact is that in American culture, and despite our cultural differences, there are many proven products and business ideas that can be adapted to the Chinese consumer market.

Remember, innovative thinking and creativity is what counts. With creativity and innovative thinking, the sky's the limit.

For anyone interested in engaging in conversation about any topic in this book or China's future, I am available as a consultant and can be reached at the email address below. The possibilities are endless, the discussions would be interesting and the results could be lucrative.

Acknowledgments:

I thank my friends and loved ones for the love and support they give me. I thank my Chinese friends who are all also my Chinese teachers. I thank my new friend, Tracy, for her hard work, attention to detail and expertise in translating this book into Chinese. I thank my cats for the times they slept, giving me time to think and time to write.

Lastly I'd like to thank Donna Casey, (Digital Donna), for once again expertly taking my crazy cover design ideas and using her talent, time and artistic vision in bringing my cover design to life.

~ Frank Silva, January 2013
(One month after the end of the world - I guess the Mayans were wrong.)

The author welcomes comments and discussion and can be reached at ShoestringVenturesLLC@gmail.com - or - Filosfrfrank@yahoo.com

About the Author

Frank Silva has a Master of Science in Education, is a former high school teacher, former police officer and high school & collegiate swimmer. He served as an officer in the U.S. Army and Army Reserves until his retirement in 2007. He has been a tour guide at Universal Studios, Florida, and has conducted educational tours at Disney's EPCOT Center and Kennedy Space Center. He holds an internationally recognized TEFL diploma and has taught English in China. He is a recreational alto saxophone player and holds a U.S. Patent as the co-inventor of a saxophone reed maintenance device. He has also been a working actor in television and film in both Florida and Los Angeles and is a member of the Screen Actors Guild - American Federation of Television and Radio Artists (SAG-AFTRA). He has appeared on television in shows such as *24*, *From the Earth to the Moon*, *Judging Amy* and *Numb3rs* and in feature films such as *Ready, Willing & Able* and *Smokin' Aces*. He is currently hard at work on the screen adaptation of his novel *The Thousand Natural Shocks*, which is available in print at Amazon.com as well as online as an e-book, and has a number of e-books online. He continues to write fiction and non-fiction and is currently working on the sequel to his *Natural Shocks* novel, *The Karmic Adventures of Shalimar & Angie*.

感谢

我要感谢我的朋友、家人和所有我爱的人,感谢他们对我的爱和支持。我要感谢我的中国朋友,他们同时还是我的中国老师。我要感谢我的新朋友,Tracy,感谢她辛勤的工作,严谨的态度以及专业的翻译技巧,把这本书翻译成中文。我还要感谢我家的猫咪们,它们的睡眠给了我时间思考和写作。

最后,我要感谢唐娜·凯西(Donna Casey,绰号数字唐娜),再一次运用她的天赋、时间和艺术家的视觉把我那疯狂的封面设计要求转化为现实。

Frank Silva
2013 年 1 月
(传说中的世界末日后的一个月——估计玛雅人错了)

任何评价和建议,请以电邮形式与作者联系:
ShoestringVenturesLLC@gmail.com 或者
filosfrfrank@yahoo.com

关于作者

Frank Silva 拥有教育学理学硕士学位,曾担任高中老师和警官,还是高中以及大学的游泳运动员。

他在美国陆军（U.S. Army）和美国陆军后备队（Army Reserves）里面担任军官，直到 2007 年退休。他是总部在美国加州的环球影业（Universal Studios）的一名导游，他还组织过到艾波卡特（EPCOT，美国佛罗里达州奥兰多华特迪士尼世界度假区里的一个主题公园）和肯尼迪航天中心（Kennedy Space Center）的教育游历。他拥有国际英语教师资格证书（TEFL）并在中国从事英语教学。他是业余中音萨克斯演奏者，合作发明了一套保养萨克斯簧片的工具，并且因此获得美国专利。他在佛罗里达州和洛杉矶两个地方做过电视剧和电影演员，他还是美国电影电视演员工会（Screen Actors Guild - American Federation of Television and Radio Artists[SAG-AFTRA]）的会员。他曾出演过的美剧有《24》、《从地球到月球》（*From the Earth to the Moon*）、《女法官艾米》（*Judging Amy*），和《数字追凶》（*Numb3rs*），电影有《*Ready, Willing & Able*》和《呛烟高手》（*Smokin' Aces*）。目前他正努力把他的小说《*The Thousand Natural Shocks*》改编为电影剧本，这本小说在亚马逊有印刷版发售，在其他网站有电子版，他还有其他一些电子书著作。他一直撰写小说与纪实文学作品，目前正在编写他的 *Natural Shocks* 系列小说的续集和新作《*The Karmic Adventures of Shalimar & Angie*》。

FRANK SILVA

东西相遇

为何中国经济前景光明且将成为 21世纪全球领袖

*****

这不是一本关于政治或政治意识形态的书，也不探讨资本主义与共产主义孰优孰劣。它没有描述中美文化差异，也没有涉及历史上的伟大帝国及其统治的兴衰与成败。

这本书甚至还没有涉及中国现行的混合式经济体制，在共产主义国家里实行资本主义经济制度，甚至运行得比美国还好。从各个方面看，中国已经成为世界领先的资本主义经济国家，在世界历史上最成功地运行资本主义经济制度。尽管这种混合式经济体制或许是今天世界金融和经济讨论的一个重要话题，我们把它叫做共产主义和资本主义的结合（capitacommunism），可是在这本书里我们没有讨论。

此外，许多著名学者，企业家和经济学家已经反复写过这方面内容的书籍，包括对中国商业的理解，如何在中国做生意，如何与中国做生意，中国企业和工厂的情况等等。还有很多其他著作是关于企业管理和经济的方方面面，以及它们如何运用到中国的实际情况中来，仿佛中国是在离西方国家很远的星球中一样，需要大量的著作和研究。我曾经读过一个作者在 2001 年出版的书，他指出在 2006 年中国的经济会彻底崩溃。我写这本书是在 2012 年，虽然我不是很肯定，但我想他应该是错了。等等，让我看一看窗外，是的，他错了。

不过把玩笑放一边，我对那个作家还是很尊重的，虽然他错了。我们先不要考虑以上所有的想法和比较，也不要考虑我用来对中国未来进行分析和推断的因素，讨论和例子，这本书是纯粹讲商业和历史的。

更加具体一点，这本书是讲述美国20世纪的经济状况，以及美国如何崛起成为全球经济领袖。这样的历史在很多其他地方都有发生，现在是轮到中国成为全球领袖的时候了，它具体是如何在本世纪上半叶发展的，这本书将为你娓娓道来。

我的伟大的祖国已经衰落了，如果说我没有为此感到难过，那是骗人的。对于近些年特别是9·11以后我的祖国所做的一些选择，我同样感到伤心。然而，目睹中国在世界范围内的经济崛起，我作为学习历史的人又是感到那么的有意思和激动人心。

记住这一点，那些国家间的相互控制、影响、或者权力争夺等政治意识形态都不是我感兴趣的。我不会写关于政治斗争的东西。只有这个地球以及居住在它里面的人才是我感兴趣的。这个地球物资丰富，默默地为我们以及所有人（所有国家）提供一切所需。在全球范围内，我们只需要那些亿万富翁和政客们多为这个星球和人们着想，真诚地为地球环境和其他生物考虑就够了，他们应该开始像负责任的成人而不是像学校操场上被宠坏的小屁孩那样思考和行动了。

　　这里有一个美国宇航员第一次在太空环绕地球的故事。太空船围绕地球转一圈需要90分钟。这位宇航员说，在第一天，每次太空船飞到他的家乡上空，大概每隔一个半小时，他都要看一看窗外。接下来就只飞到他的州时才看，再后来到他生活的那片区域才看，再后来他就只看美国了。没过几天他就把地球看成一个整体，再也不去特别看哪一块了。

　　当我第一次听见这个故事时我就说，如果可以把每一个大国领导都放到太空船里去环绕地球就五天的时间，那就好了，这个世界可能就会变得更美好一些。

　　我会建议让那些世界级富翁也去坐一坐飞船。可是，我相信他们大部分都只会把地球看成是他们的财产或者能够用财富征服和控制的地方，而不会想到这是一个家，一个所有地球人共同拥有和分享的家。

　　在不可能把他们送到外太空的前提下，我们也只能接受目前的状况。

　　一群伟大的中产阶级在20世纪诞生，并为美国的繁荣作出了不可缺少的贡献，然而那些贪婪的亿万富翁以及他们控制的财团却有意地将这一切摧毁，我感到非常伤心。

同时这也是对美国经济和工人阶级中产阶级的一次致命打击。

然而，美国的坏事对中国来说却是好事。美国的衰落部分地成就了中国今天的繁荣，并且不久的将来把中国变成世界的领导。

关键在于中国*有*很多人。

不幸的是，中国也有很多穷人。

在规模上跟美国相比，恐怕这个难题不容易解决。我相信今天的美国有跟中国一样多甚至更多的穷人。不同点在于，在美国我们只有 3 亿人口，因此穷人的数量会远远比中国的 14 亿人口里的穷人少。

除此之外，中国要实现繁荣富强并跃居为全球经济强国，庞大的人口是一个关键因素。

中国将来要走的路是显而易见的，庞大的人口基数不仅提供劳力，还提供强大的消费市场，这个因素不得不考虑。

美国 20 世纪走过的路给 21 世纪的中国指明了通往繁荣富强的方向，中国只需要沿着这条路走下去，就可以给中国人民带来丰衣足食。勤勤恳恳的中国人，每一天都努力争取为自己和所爱的人过上更好地生活，他们的愿望终究会实现。

在这里，我并没有说我有所有问题的答案，不过我相信我的想法对在中国做生意的人很有帮助，并且非常重要。我在这里给睿智的中国商界精英们指明了通往繁荣兴旺的方向。

我还想要提醒你们我写这本书是在2012年，这时候世界局势相对稳定。在排除一切特殊情况，例如世界大战，全球范围的环境灾难，瘟疫，或者包括中国在内的全球经济衰退，我相信这是中国未来要走的路。

排除了这样或那样灾难发生的可能，接下来中国十有八九会走上繁荣富强的路，并成为全球领袖。

交过接力棒

在接力赛跑中，拿着接力棒的运动员以最快速度逼近下一个运动员。下一个运动员在等待队友的同时，估计队友的速度，开始小跑起来，不时地回头看队友，伸出他的手，手掌向上，随时迎接身后队友追上他的一霎，把接力棒交到他手中。接下来这个运动员就成为田径场上的主角，用尽全力向前冲。

我们可以拿这个例子与历史上众多庞大帝国的兴衰史相比。这些帝国往往都是充满自信，认为自己所向披靡，慢慢变得高傲自大，开始自我毁灭。不幸的是，它们当中的很多，都嗜权如命，用尽各种不光彩的手段去维持和拓展它们的权力。

尽管如此，我们只需要稍微搜索一下历史，就能找到这些强国们是如何式微，在什么时候把自己的政权拱手相让给下一个统治者。

例如，古罗马帝国是历史上最伟大的国家之一。这个国家曾经拥有该时代前所未有的科技成就，他们有最先进的道路桥梁和发达的下水道排污系统。可是它终究衰落，没有存活到今天。不幸的是，古罗马帝国和现代的美国有很多相同之处。

在近代现代史里，许多欧洲国家为权力和领土发动战争，相继成为世界霸主。（他们所认为的世界。）当时出现了一些非常强大，非常富有，非常有影响力的大国如西班牙和法国。在这本书里，我只需要追朔到 19 世纪的大不列颠帝国，看看当时的英国是如何"统治"那个世界的。

在近代史里，大不列颠帝国是当时世界上最繁荣和最具影响力的国家。中国人还记得香港曾经是它的殖民地，当时的上海也深深地受到英国的影响。

很明显，大不列颠是当时世界上占支配地位的国家，并且即使在美国独立战争中失去了美国这一块重要的殖民地后，它仍然是当时数一数二的国家。（顺便说一句，如果没有法国的帮忙，美国独立战争不会成功，历史上法国一直是英国的死对头。为此，我会一直感谢法国以及法国人民。今天，美国仍然欠了法国很多。没有法国的帮忙就没有今天的美国。太多的美国人忘记了这一点，却记住了美国如何在20世纪的世界大战中解放了法国。）

到19世纪末，由于过度扩张，大不列颠帝国花费了难以估计的财富，已经难以维持它的政权了。它的很多殖民地开始寻求独立。在20世纪初的第一次世界大战中花费的巨额金钱更是成为英帝国最后的致命一击。

第一次世界大战以后接力棒开始交到了美国手上。尽管当时有30年代的大萧条，但这都不能影响美国日益膨胀的势力。其中有几年的时间，英国和美国非常亲密地合作在一起解决中东问题，两个国家都分到了相应的势力范围，但是很明显英国在衰落而美国在壮大。第二次世界大战同盟军的胜利，以及美国研发出了第一颗原子弹，都很大程度地推动美国当仁不让地坐上世界的头把交椅。

从那时候开始，美国就成为世界霸主。实际上，我在写这本书的时候，美国依然是世界霸主。然而，我相信这种情况会有所改变，而接力棒会在21世纪传到中国手上。

没有人能准确地预言什么时候会发生，但我猜测这个过程已经开始并且会在以后的十到二十年的时间内发生。

现在我就在这本书里告诉你们第一个秘密：中国不需要西方。西方国家却需要中国。要成为世界霸主，中国不需要任何一个国家的帮助。超乎所有人的想象，今天的中国完全可以实现自给自足，走向独立和繁荣。很多中国人认为西方拥有最先进的技术，因此他们在商业和经济领域占有优势。在2012年这可能还算有道理，但是知识分子、天才和有创意的人哪里都有，美国以及西方，哪里都没有对这种人才进行垄断。从历史和科学技术的角度看，西方和美国也许有那么一点点的优势，可是世界正在改变，科技日新月异，世界上每一个角落都有新的研究和新的技术面世。今天中国拥有很多得天独厚的优势，地域辽阔，人口众多，资源丰富，还是世界制造业中心，这些优势使得中国避免了美国的经济衰退和西方国家面临的经济难题。

在我列举的世界各国接力赛例子中，这位中国选手已经开始迈出了他的步伐，他正在加速前进，急切地等待着接力棒交到他手中。

建立消费型社会

像美国一样建立起一个消费型社会，能够对国家的发展带来巨大裨益。

无论是国内需求还是出口贸易，都带动着整个国家的经济发展，这一点所有国家都一样。消费刺激制造业生产更多产品，提供更多工作岗位和薪水给工人，这些工人再拿着这些薪水去买生活必需品和他们想要的服务。记住，工人们会在两种事物上花钱，一是生活必需品，二是满足精神层面的物品和服务。

美国的消费型社会促进经济的繁荣发展，造就了一大批富裕的工人阶级和中产阶级。

消费不是一件坏事，然而，过度消费就不是好事，并且有可能走向毁灭。关键在于以理性的消费维持经济的增长，而不至于转变成毁灭性的过度消费阶段。只要听从经济学家的指导，耐心地教导消费者谨慎考虑每一次消费选择，养成良好的消费习惯，这样过度消费就不会出现。

我相信美国已经经历了繁荣的消费市场所带来的经济腾飞，也经历了下一个毁灭性的过度消费阶段。我没有把这个恶果责怪到美国人民头上，相反，我觉得是那些追求经济利益最大化的大集团公司的错，还有那些永远乐意借钱给人们的银行，是它们把这些人推向永无止境的债务当中。

我相信是这些公司和银行导致了毁灭性消费。那些公司不断地追求更高的销售和利润，人们不断地被银行灌输一时的享乐是值得终生债务的价值观，二者结合在一起形成了更具有毁灭性的效果。

在美国，大部分中产阶级家庭里都有车库。然而今天的美国，车库都不是用来放车的，而是用来作储物室，放满很多美国人买的"物品"。这些物品很快就被新的物品取代，久而久之家里就没有放这些旧物品的空间了。很多美国人在他们车库里放满很多不用、不需要和不想要的物品，还有更多美国人把更多的这些物品放在公共储物室。目前在美国，以出售像车库一样的空间来存放物品的服务非常受欢迎，私人公司会把这些空间锁起来保护好。听起来好像不可思议，可是现在在美国这样的储物公司随处可见，并且生意好得很，通常都是租满的。人们每个月都花钱租这些空间来放他们攒起来的不再需要的物品，可是他们又不忍心把物品卖掉或者扔掉。

另外，每到夏天，很多社区里的家庭都会组织一次车库物品集市，人们把自己不想要的东西放在屋前的草坪上卖给别家的人。有时候人们可以在这样的集市用很便宜的价钱买到自己需要或想要的东西，有时候人们又可以卖掉一些闲置物品，买进一些其他物品。通常，人们卖掉他们不想要的东西，却又买回别人不想要的东西替代他们原来的东西。然后他们回家用新买回来的旧东西填满好不容易腾出来的车库的空间。这听起来简直难以理解，好像我在开玩笑，虽然我也有一点开他们玩笑的成分，但这一切都是真的。

过度消费还包括对食品的过度消费，导致美国变成世界上拥有最多肥人的国家。事实证明对食品的过度消费已经产生毁灭性的结果，例如健康问题引起高昂的医药费和寿命缩短。

**

理性消费可以刺激国家经济，对中国来说，它会为中国带来持续的经济增长和繁荣。理性消费不但为人们提供工作，还允许人们买到他们想要或者需要的东西，比如不同类型的衣服、手机、电脑、家用电器和所有其它能为人们带来舒适和便利的生活的东西，这会大大提高人们的生活水平。

有着 14 亿消费者的中国，它的经济可以发展得比历史上任一个西方国家更快更强。

企业经营与增长

影响经济增长的因素有很多。

我无意在这里一一阐述，也不想变成大学的经济学教程。我想在这里介绍一些企业领导和创业者可以用到的实用的观点，去帮助他们做决定，帮助他们取得成功，最终让自己和家人过上更好地生活。

记住了这一点，我就可以向你们介绍一些有所启发的例子。每一家企业都想提高业务量。要提高利润，做大做强，提高业务量是必需的。

然而，所有事情都有一个度。

关于业务增长的度的问题，这里有一个来自美国快餐业的很好的例子。

美国人把麦当劳，KFC 和必胜客带到中国来，对此我先在这里向大家道歉。这些洋快餐在中国可能很流行，并且味道也不差，却为肥胖症、糖尿病和心脏病的发生埋下了隐患。他们为美国人带来不健康的生活方式，现在漂洋过海来到中国继续做同样的事。另外，比萨是我最钟爱的食物之一，如果吃得适度，它是没有害的。然而，必胜客，就连美国的，都不能叫做比萨。在美国，那些注重食物营养的人，比如我，是不会蠢到相信那些纯粹误导的广告，我们甚至不会拿麦当劳和必胜客的东西去喂狗。

好了，关于我对快餐没味道没营养的观点就说到这里为止。

**

第二次世界大战后不久创立的美国快餐业，是一个绝顶聪明的商业概念。

这些快餐店的创始人都有一个理念，就是每一家餐厅都可以被复制成很多家分店，并确保每一家都有一模一样的食物和服务。

这个理念可以使喜欢纽约某一家餐厅的客人，可以在迈阿密或洛杉矶等其他城市的任一家分店尝到同样的食物，例如汉堡包。

这个理念很受欢迎，快餐连锁店都把他们的分店开遍全国，成为全国性企业。

T这样快餐业的竞争就很激烈了。在美国我们有很多快餐店。麦当劳自成立之日起就是美国快餐业的领军企业，但它也受到其他餐厅的挑战，这些后起之秀包括汉堡王，Wendy's和很多其他还没有进军中国市场的西方品牌。

这些快餐店都发展成为家喻户晓的全国性的品牌。

这时候，好玩的事情发生了。在它们不断争夺市场份额，争夺客源的过程中，它们尝试了很多不同的策略。其中大部分的策略都很见效，其他快餐店也在激烈的竞争中相互模仿。

举个例子：一家餐厅提供的儿童套餐里面附带一个小玩具。其他的公司纷纷模仿。那么一家公司就会跟一部流行的儿童电影或电视节目签约，要求他们提供里面的人物作为套餐附带的毛绒公仔。接下来每一家公司都会疯狂地找著名卡通人物和电影电视角色合作，这样家长就可以带小孩过来吃饭，同时得到一个额外的玩具。

把具体的市场策略放一边，我想你们把注意力集中到这个竞争激烈的市场的成长概念中。

首先，这些快餐店提供午餐和晚餐。当人们上班的时候，吃快餐作午餐很受欢迎，这是一个巨大的市场。晚餐则相对受冷落，因为很多人都回家，跟家人吃晚餐。

因为美国人开始过上快节奏的生活，也因为越来越多的家庭主妇不再呆在家而出来工作，她们没有时间准备晚餐，这时，吃快餐作晚餐也开始在美国流行起来。

在午餐和晚餐的双重份额下，快餐业稳定地持续增长。

一旦他们开始达到增长的极限，光靠午餐和晚餐的销售已经不能满足他们对增长的需求，他们必需找新的办法去增加收入，毕竟只有那么多消费者，也只有两顿饭，午餐和晚餐。

这时，有人发明了超大分量这个做法。现在，消费者只要多给一点点钱，就可以把原来的汉堡包，薯条和汽水都加大一个分量，他们都愿意这样做。

很快，超大分量成为典型的快餐。

然而快餐店们又一次到达增长极限。

为了能继续增长，他们推出了早餐，一个全新的品种和全新的市场。

我不是很肯定哪一个出现比较早，是早餐呢还是超大分量，不过这都不是很重要。重要的是它们都是为贡献销售持续增长而采取的策略。

早餐市场的竞争同午餐晚餐一样激烈。随着越来越多的人在他们工作或上学的路上吃快餐式早餐，很多人的午餐也选择快餐，所有快餐公司都繁荣兴旺起来。

毫无疑问快餐很方便，节省了找合适食物的时间和精力。取决于人们选择什么品牌和吃多少，快餐也可以很廉价。

尽管竞争异常激烈，所有快餐公司都保持增长，每年都有几十亿美元的收入，可是很快老问题又出现了，他们都快要达到增长的极限，新的策略必须尽快想出来以维持增速。

最近我阅读了很多关于快餐业的市场营销策略的材料，我又再一次为我的祖国感到悲伤，感慨那些大公司和企业如何操纵我们的文化。

随着快餐业增长达到极限，他们已经无计可施，现在他们正在尝试向美国公众推销"第四顿饭"。

在我们乃至世界大部分地方的传统文化里，我们会吃三顿饭——早餐，午餐和晚餐。为了保持不断的增长，快餐业的领导者开始尝试*重新教育*美国人，特别是美国小孩，向他们灌输在晚餐后睡觉前吃第四顿饭的观念。

一天四顿饭真是荒唐至极，可是如果那些市场营销专家成功了，正如他们通常都会，那么美国小孩在成长过程中就会被灌输第四顿饭是个好主意，久而久之就形成习惯，觉得吃三顿饭才不正常。这恐怕又会成为人为加到我们文化中的又一个不良饮食习惯。

我把它看成是又一个扭曲的消费主义的例子，它说明了大公司追求利益最大化是多么具有毁灭性。

人们不需要一天四顿饭，很多人连三顿都没有，一些人甚至两顿都不能保证，还有很多人没有运气找到一丁点食物。

不管怎样，重点是快餐业为了寻求无止境的增长，已经江郎才尽了，才发明这么一个全新的市场。

**

把这一点跟中国联系起来——对于所有的产品和服务，中国的消费市场是14亿消费者的市场。这个庞大的市场还没有被开发，中国还处于消费型社会的婴儿时期。

因此，今天中国大部分的商品和服务都有无限的市场增长潜力，这会给中国带来令人咂舌的经济增长和市场繁荣，最终会大大提高大部分中国人的生活水平，促使中国崛起成为世界第一强国。记住这一点，即使是平庸的销售业绩，放在中国庞大的消费市场中，也有潜力成为美国鼎盛时期市场销售的三到四倍。

语言和文化及其在世界的影响，美国霸权

为什么世界上大部分人都说英语？为什么那么多中国人学英语？

我知道很多中国人学英语是因为，中国是世界工厂，很多跟中国做生意的外国人都说英语。

世界上最多人使用的三种语言是汉语，英语和西班牙语。

It 很容易就能看出来为什么汉语这么重要，被这么多人使用。

学习历史也可以告诉我们为什么西班牙语如此重要。

　　西班牙曾是一个伟大的帝国，它征服了很多新的陆地和岛屿，变成其殖民地。那些陆地和岛屿后来建立了新的国家，因此，大部分在中南美洲和北美洲的墨西哥都讲西班牙语。

　　正是因为很多移民到美国的新居民都来自拉丁美洲，所以美国有一大部分人口都说西班牙语。专家估计到本世纪中叶，在美国讲西班牙语的人会超过讲英语的人。

　　葡萄牙帝国也曾派出远征队探索新世界，他们征服了南美洲最大的国家——巴西，因此这个国家讲葡萄牙语。巴西是一个贸易大国，他们把工厂设在中国，但是中国工厂和巴西公司做生意用的却是英语。

　　为什么？

　　20世纪的美国崛起成为世界强国之前，英国建立了强大的帝国，征服了全世界包括亚洲的很多地方。作为英国的殖民地，亚洲很多国家都实行英语教育。

　　然而，促使英语成为主流语言，特别是广泛应用于国际贸易，则是由于二战后的美国崛起。（这里说一点题外话，美国的势力同时也确保了美元成为世界储备货币。可是，由于近年来的美国金融困境频繁出现，特别是2008年的金融危机，使得很多国家开始用不同国家的货币来取代单一的美元储备。再者，一些国家也开始直接用他们自己国家的货币来取代美元做国际贸易。）

英语在国际贸易的地位一时还不会动摇。

然而，我相信在本世纪，汉语会变成一门更加重要的语言在全球范围内使用。因为很多人还在说西班牙语，因此西班牙语还是很重要。在本世纪，汉语和英语将会相互竞争成为全球最有影响力的语言，广泛应用于国际贸易。

在欧洲，很多人讲多种语言。欧洲的面积相对较小，却有如此多的国家。由于贸易往来的需要，欧洲人有必要学习多种语言，这种做法很聪明。

由于很多不同原因，美国人很大程度地忽略了外来文化和语言。一部分原因是我之前有提到过的，美国人太高傲。在整个20世纪的大部分时间，美国人都有这种感觉，因为我们是世界各国的嫉妒对象，我们是世界上最强大的国家，很多人学习我们的语言。

这一切都是真的。正因为这样，美国人不再学习其他文化和语言。直到今天美国人才意识到他们错了。可是却很少有人试图去改变这种状况。

当我们逐渐深入到21世纪时，有一件重要的事情要记住，那就是如果一个人会讲汉语或者英语，无论谁，特别是与做生意挂上钩的人，都将会对他们有很大好处。如果一个人会说汉语和英语，那么他得到的好处会更多，会比任何人都走得都远。如果一个人会说汉语，英语和西班牙语，那他在这个地球上基本是无所不能了。

（我没有说到阿拉伯语，尽管在今天这是一门很重要的语言。很多中东国家都说阿拉伯语，尽管范围很小并且会变得越来越小。我相信随着石油时代的结束，大部分中东国家会没有那么重要，在不久的将来会失去权力。我相信如果西方和亚洲国家不再搀和这些中东国家的内政，他们就不会再和西方抗衡。因此，阿拉伯语就不是一门那么有必要学的语言，肯定也不够汉语，英语和西班牙语那么重要了。还有最后一门有可能变得重要的语言就是俄语，不过这要取决于将来俄罗斯在世界中的地位。）

美国崛起简史

在19世纪末，大不列颠帝国开始衰落。就像历史上没落的帝国一样，它的领土过度扩张，其统治下的殖民地陆续寻求独立和自由。与此同时,美国也因为把势力伸向海外而开始崛起成为世界强国。

第一次世界大战实际上把英国正式推向破产。这次大战中,美国并没有马上加入战争,而是保存实力,随时准备应战。当美国正式宣战时,局势已经基本明朗,美国的加入加快了德国的溃败。

历史上的这个时候,新的发明,比如飞机和坦克,已经开始影响战争的打法,更是因为如此,石油变得非常重要。

由于地下蕴藏大量原油,中东地区的战略地位也变得很重要。随着英国的衰落,美国开始控制中东地区。在很短一段时间里,美国和英国亲密地合作起来,共同控制中东国家及其能源。

这也诱发了到今天还不能解决的问题。伊拉克的国界是由英国决定的。问题在于这个国家有三种不同的文化和族群,逊尼派穆斯林(Sunni Muslim),什叶派穆斯林(Shiite Muslims)和库尔德人(Kurds)。

什叶派穆斯林人数最多,库尔德族人其次。英国和美国为首的西方势力却与逊尼派穆斯林达成协议,答应支持势力弱小的逊尼派穆斯林以换取廉价的石油。因此尽管逊尼派穆斯林人数最少,它组成的伊拉克政府却有英美的军事力量在背后撑腰。

这只是其中一个由石油政治引起的国际问题。

自从很多有影响力和富有的美国人从一战出来后变得更加有影响力和富有，他们开始对全球经济和其他全球性事件指手画脚。

这个直接导致了我们叫做"咆哮的二十年代"（roaring twenties），指的是20世纪20年代的美国。这段时期美国经济命脉由最富有的美国人掌控，有美国政府做后台，他们开始为所欲为。金融和商业发展速度惊人，华尔街的股市节节上升，一派繁荣。

这时美国的经济几乎脱离政府干预，很多有钱人变得更加有钱。

然而，美国这种不规范的经济运行，以及部分大公司的不道德行为，最终导致1929年全球股市崩盘。

这次股灾标志着经济大萧条的开始，接下来的1929到1933年，美国及全世界的经济雪上加霜。

20世纪30年代，美国总统富兰克林·德拉诺·罗斯福（Franklin Delano Roosevelt）下令通过了更多规范金融商业的法律，减小他们对国家经济的毁灭性影响。同时他还用纳税人的钱启动了不少项目，投资国家建设，试图把国家和人民从大萧条的极度贫困中拉出来。

在这段时期，我们修建了新路和新桥，还有其他国家基础设施。他还发起了社会保障制度，使工薪族在退休后有一笔固定的退休金，能够安享晚年。

在 30 年代，这些措施都起了一定的效果，但大萧条的杀伤力还是巨大的。我们那时有很多穷人，无家可归者和无业游民。

然而，美国那些有影响力的企业家和政客已经知道，到 30 年代中期，一场新的世界大战即将来临。

没有人喜欢战争。战争对纳税人来说是一笔巨大的开支，它摧毁家园，涂炭生灵，伤害成千上万无辜的老百姓。不幸的是，那些有权有势的人往往从中获利，他们是战争的怂恿者和支持者。有钱的公司老板是唯一喜欢战争的人，因为他们能够安全地获得非常高的利润，远离战场和死亡。

在 30 年代的二战期间，美国的战争策略再次重复一战时的做法，在战争开始时先观望不行动，同时做好各方面的准备，把国内各个行业的位置调整好，以便一参战就能从中获得最大利益。(这里又提一点题外话，二战期间有一部分有钱人服了兵役，在越南战争中大部分的有钱人逃避了服兵役，包括乔治·W·布什[George W. Bush]，今天，*没有*有钱人费心去履行任何兵役，尽管他们口口声声说"爱国"。）

尽管当时日本已经侵入很多国家如中国，打响了太平洋这边的战争，而德国也于1939年9月正式入侵波兰，宣告二战正式开始，美国却迟迟不肯宣战，直到它完全准备好。

实际上，当时美国参议员，未来的总统哈里·杜鲁门（Harry Truman）已经表态说美国应该等尽可能长时间，看谁有战胜的苗头（德国和俄罗斯之间），之后才能参与战争，这样在美国加入之前各国的人都死得差不多了。

最后，美国的领导们和战略家们终于选定了一边并且计划参战了。最容易进入的方法就是迫使日本主动进攻美国，这样美国就有借口宣战了。（虽然我们大部分的历史都少不了战争和冲突，但是在美国文化里，我们还是喜欢说服自己美国是一个热爱和平国家，除了最近在中东和中亚国家的问题上，我们扮演侵略者的角色之外，我们总是试着令其他国家迫不得已先进攻我们，于是我们就声称站在道德高地上光荣地迎战，并且相信我们有足够理由"报复"他们的"攻击"。）

即使我们没有向德国、意大利和日本组成的轴心国开战，美国却用尽各种办法切断日本急需的能源供应。这使得日本要么走向资源衰竭的地步，失掉这场战争，要么攻击美国以获取石油。

我不会详细阐述二战历史，我们都知道结果。

唯一值得我一提的是，美国有幸比德国更早开发出原子弹。要是德国早一步研发出原子弹，那么这场战争会有完全不同的结果，对美国还是中国都不是好事。

**

在二战*后*发生的事情对中国有特别重要的意义，很可能是中国在21世纪走向繁荣富强的蓝图。

接近二战尾声，大部分的欧洲已经被摧毁，德国的大部分工厂，虽然不是全部，和很多城市也毁于一旦。

历史上的这段时间，亚洲国家，特别是中国，还处于欠发达状态，没有任何新科技成就出现。

凭着众多工厂日以继夜地生产各种战时物资和材料，美国自然地成为世界工厂。于是美国停止生产战时物资，转向生产消费产品。举个例子，汽车制造厂在战争期间生产吉普车，坦克和飞机，而不是汽车。战争之后，这些工厂就返回到以前的汽车生产中。

接下来的美国历史才是中国人需要集中注意力的重要部分。

当时的美国主要依赖出口贸易。由于销售和利润的提高，美国工人有充足的就业机会和不断增长的薪水。有了更多的自由支配的金钱，美国人开始要求更多的消费品来满足他们的需求。

一个工厂的美国人不只是为其他国家的人生产这些产品，同时为另一个美国工厂的工人生产这些产品。

这个循环不断进行着，提高了美国人的生活水平。这使得很多美国人实实在在地成为中产阶级，拿着中产阶级应该拿的薪水。我们的中产阶级人数大大提高，国家和人民极大地富裕起来。我们成为一个更加富裕的国家——"更加富裕的国家"我指的是工人阶级、中产阶级以及那些公司企业都同时富裕起来，在这段繁荣时期，公司企业的收入和利润都很大程度地提升。

这段时期一直延续到 50 年代，美国人过上了富足和快乐的生活。

踏入 60 年代，从经济上看，美国人依然享受着十年的经济繁荣，但同时也被一些社会不稳定因素困扰着。卷入越南战争，黑人和妇女这两个当时（现在仍是）广泛受到歧视的弱势群体开始站出来维护自己的权益，这些都构成了美国非常艰苦的十年。我们的总统约翰·肯尼迪（John F. Kennedy）在 1963 年被刺杀。接下来的 1968 年，他的弟弟罗伯特·肯尼迪（Bobby Kennedy）在总统竞选中也遭刺杀。同一年，美国史上伟大的民权运动领袖马丁·路德·金（）也遭毒手，他毕生为黑人争取应有的权利，还终止了越南战争。相比之下，在 1969 年，美国宇航员则第一次成功地走在月球上。

这是困难的、兴奋的、又是活跃的十年，从很多方面改变了美国发展的历程。

在这段期间，更多的妇女出来工作。一方面是因为她们开始追求独立，另一方面也是因为对很多家庭来说，光靠一份收入已经不足够应付所有开支了。

美国仍然很富裕，可是其他国家，如日本，已经开始制造出更多的产品出口到国外了。

由于美国工人的薪水不断增长，国外劳力却相对廉价，因此日本出口到美国的产品可以卖到更低价钱，这种情况开始对美国的制造业有所影响。

70 年代是我们国家经济发展的转折点，特别是对美国工人来说，更是重要的转折。

在 70 年代，随着能源价格的提高，原材料成本和制造业一起继续增长。公司企业继续获得利润的同时也提高销售价格来弥补成本的上升。然而，各大公司开始放缓工资的增速，工人们薪水的提升并没有跟原料成本、产品销售价格和公司利润同步。

美国的工人不再有足够的钱支付日常开支以及购买他们需要和想要的消费品和服务了。

那时美国的生活水平已经相当高，享受生活的便利已经成为我们文化的一部分。美国人不愿意放弃这些舒服和便利。

银行看中了人们不想少买物品或者降低他们的生活质量的想法，提供了更高额更容易的贷款服务，于是，美国打工族就开始靠借钱和信用卡过日子。被企业鼓吹的消费主义计划所推动，银行家们想让人们知道他们是可以轻松地购买任何他们想要的东西，然后方便地在将来一点一点偿还。但是他们不想让人们知道贷款的真相，更不想人们感到焦虑，银行收取的利息会随着时间越攒越多，附加在物品的价格上，这个物品就比原价贵多了。人们选择贷款购买的物品通常是电视机和厨房电器，比如烤箱和搅拌器，还有所有其他提高生活舒适度的用具。

美国人开始习惯性地用信用卡购买东西，而信用卡公司和银行是恨不得提供更多的信用额度。债务开始在 70 年代积累起来，到了 80 年代，很多美国人已经变得负债累累。

此外，尽管我们有最低工资标准，但美国工人们还是不能摆脱滚雪球般的债务。

最低工资一开始是参考贫困线制定出来的。贫困线是最低的生活标准，只能保证一个全职工人非常基本的生活必需品如住房、食物、衣服、交通和有限的医疗服务。美国最低工资的制定应该是按照这一套理论来的，可是随着原材料成本的上升，企业们也提高产品价格以达到相同的利润提升幅度，最低工资却没有跟上公司利润或者产品价格提高的幅度。举个例子，今天的最低工资是大概 7 美元一个小时，可是根据经济学家的说法，如果按照过去几十年物价的飙升和企业盈利的增长速度，最低工资应该在每小时 18 到 20 美元才算是跟上它们的步伐。

令美国人雪上加霜的是，中国对外资企业特别是美国企业的开放，使得那些美国公司表面上说如何如何爱国，实际上把他们的财富隐藏在国外，钻我们法律的漏洞，逃税漏税。他们还把工厂都搬到中国，纯粹为了节省成本，而不顾这样做对美国和美国工人的负面影响。

把工厂都搬到中国却对中国及其打工族非常有利。很不幸中国工人的收入很低，这也是美国企业把工厂搬到这里的原因。中国庞大的劳动力急需工作，哪怕只有那么一点点的回报也心甘情愿，美国企业就是看到了这一点。他们甚至连*这一点点*回报都不愿意给，想方设法压榨工人，能*不给*就不给。（算他们不走运，大部分国家都取缔了奴隶制。）

看见自己工作的工厂关闭，转移到中国，美国工人的日子过得更加艰苦（同时，墨西哥也面临同一局面）。

问题就在于美国工人们只能继续靠信用卡以及二战后经济繁荣时期他们攒下的那么一点点积蓄过活。

对 70 年代的美国工人来说，他们只能耗尽所有积蓄，越来越依赖信用卡，从银行借更多的钱，欠了一身债。而这些日益增长的债务继续推动美国消费型社会的发展长达 15 到 20 年。到了 90 年代，问题开始浮出水面，更大的问题在新世纪爆发了。

在 80 年代，更多的工作岗位转移到中国和其他发展中国家。

为了不断增长的利润，美国的亿万富翁和他们的企业关掉在美国的工厂，撤出美国，断送了千千万万美国人的工作。他们把企业转到中国，牺牲了美国工人阶级和中产阶级的利益。他们不在乎他们的国家，只关心自己和他们企业的利益，到今天还是。

（在美国，这些企业没有交过任何形式的税款，甚至连他们自己和企业直接使用或从中获益的公用设施都不用纳税。）

90年代的某一个时期开始，美国企业对世界经济有非常大的影响力。各公司雇佣专业的游说人士，他们深入政府，影响立法。与其说政府立法，不如说企业通过这些说客制定有利于自己的政策和法律。

这样，这些企业、非常有钱的企业老板以及非常有钱的企业投资人就获得了更高的利润。再加上他们有法律后盾，保证他们和他们的企业缴纳少得多的税款。一些国际巨头公司，比如美国通用电气公司，只交每年数十亿美元利润的2%作税费。

90年代末对一些银行业和金融业的关键法律的改动，为本世纪头十年的世界性经济危机埋下了伏笔。

今天，那些亿万富翁和他们控制的企业就像是美国和整个世界的寄生虫一样，他们拿走的远远比贡献的多。他们已经摧毁了美国和很多其他国家的经济，包括很多欧洲国家。

那些有权有势的亿万富翁和他们控制的企业，在英语中常常用"大到不能倒（too big to fail）"来形容。他们利用手上的财富和权力控制政府，干扰立法。政府有责任立法监督企业的不良商业行为，企业们却认为这是政府对他们的干预，并想尽一切方法抵制和改变政府的立法。他们操纵金融法律法规，制造房地产泡沫并最终导致泡沫破灭。他们控制下的银行，很容易地贷款给没有能力还款的打工族，欺骗他们房产只升不降，最终房地产泡沫破灭，引发华尔街股市危机，导致全球金融市场爆发了 2008 年的金融风暴。

  在美国的资本主义制度下，企业家们相信要是他们挣了钱要归他们所有，要是他们亏损了，那么政府应该用打工人民缴纳的税款去给他们买单，帮助他们摆脱困境。他们实在太有钱和有权了，他们可以不用去坐牢，几乎不用交税，亏了有政府垫，而广大的美国人民一点办法也没有。

  毫无疑问，现在的美国正在走下坡路。倚着有钱而横行霸道的大公司大企业不纳税，挣了归自己，亏了算政府，操纵政府立法，可怜的美国人民欠债累累，很多人没有工作，很多人连找到工作的希望都没有，再加上出奇昂贵的军事开支，美国到处煽风点火的军事策略使得军事开支不断攀升，这一切都毫无疑问地预示着美国的将来：失业率高企，人们背着沉重的债务，过着没有希望的生活。

作为美国人，我爱我的祖国，可是很遗憾，这一切都是很不幸的正在发生的现实。

这一切对美国和美国人民都不是好的，可是对中国和中国人民却是好的。

中国今天的处境跟二战刚刚结束的美国非常相似。接下来在这本书里我会为大家解释中国该如何从美国的经验当中找到方向和出路，从20世纪的美国历史中找到通往繁荣富强的道路。

繁荣的消费市场给我的国家带来前所未有的富裕，可是这个消费市场已经被利用、扭曲而变得以盈利为目的，最终这种毁灭性的消费主义令我伟大的国家走向衰落，甚至毁灭。从这一点看，美国给中国上了宝贵的一课。

*

在讨论了过去和现在，我们即将要讨论未来，可是在那以前，还有一些观点和因素需要考虑。

这里是其中一些：

能源

自从工业革命以来，在19世纪和20世纪的世界历史中，能源，特别是石油，变成一个更加重要的因素。在很多国家，能源及其使用已经使得人们生活质量提高，同时也形成了一个暴利的行业。

随着装甲车的发明，如一战时的坦克，以及军事力量在二战中对飞机，坦克和补给车的依赖，能源，特别是石油，变成其中一个决定20世纪战争输赢的最重要的因素。

德国在二战中十分依赖坦克和飞机，当希特勒的军事装备慢慢把石油储备榨干，德国的气数也走到尽头，同盟国的胜利非常明显。同样，在美国宣布加入战争之前，日本已经被美国切断了能源供应而不得不袭击珍珠港，给了美国加入战争的借口，却希望能从美国手中赢得石油。幸好日本失败了，不然对美国和中国都不是好事。（虽然今天美国和中国是朋友，但是二战时两国为共同利益紧密合作，击败日本的例子还是可以好好借鉴。我希望当两国再有矛盾时，我们会记住历史上的这个时候。）

从20世纪初期到中期，美国的石油储备很充足。我们在墨西哥边境上的德克萨斯州，和俄克拉荷马州都蕴藏着丰富的石油资源。二战之后，美国鲜有能源短缺问题。充足的能源成为促进消费市场繁荣发展的因素之一，消费者们有足够的能源去使用各种各样的产品。随着我们不断提高的生活质量，直到50年代，我们都很少有缺少能源的情况。

在20世纪的下半叶,我们的消费市场变得过热,美国人开始购买更多标志高品质生活的东西。新技术和发明加剧了这种消费方式的恶化。

在50年代,家里拥有一台电视机变得非常重要。到了60年代,一台电视机已经不是什么新鲜事了,要有两台才算是比其他家庭的生活水平高一个层次。至于拥有一台彩色电视机理所当然地要比那些拥有黑白电视机的家庭优越。等到遥控器面世了,人人都想要有遥控器的电视机,没有人愿意从座位上起来走到电视机跟前换台了。

在美国,几乎所有中产阶级家庭都拥有洗衣机和干衣机、洗碗机、烤箱,和餐厨垃圾处理器。

我之所以特别提到这些家用电器,是因为美国人太爱他们的厨房了,他们的生活离不开这种舒适。他们喜欢用烤箱做曲奇饼和派,他们喜欢把脏的碟子和碗放到洗碗机里,让机器做所有工作,他们就可以看电视了,当然现在是可以上网了。他们讨厌洗衣服,他们想要衣服洗了很快就干,很快就把事情做完。我还记得我小的时候,我妈妈把衣服晾在外面的绳子上。因为住在二楼,我们家有条绳子从我们这边跨过中间的车道伸到隔壁家的二楼,她在绳子两端装上凹槽和滑轮，就可以不用下楼直接把挂好的衣服滑出去外面，在太阳底下晾干。

现在已经很难找到像这样的晾衣服的绳子了。

可是现在的中国，每家每户阳台上都有杆子，或者晾衣架来晾干洗好的衣服。

其中一部分原因是，中国是个很大的国家，有很多很多的人。这就是为什么能源在中国更加宝贵的原因。

虽然中国资源丰富，但是仍然很难满足那么多人的需求。如果每个家庭都使用更多的电器，能源将会更加缺乏。

技术对解决这个问题很有帮助，中国也正走在正确的方向上。

世界不断进步，越来越多的替代能源正在被开发。太阳能、风能、水能，这些都越来越多地被开发用在消费品上。最近，一个悬浮式的风能涡轮机已经在葡萄牙海边做了测试，它可以移动，并且能在任何海岸抛锚。如果它没有开始商业化生产了，那它很快就会。

今天，让中国家庭用上干衣机还是不切实际，可是一旦家庭消费品如太阳能干衣机普及起来，每个家庭都能负担得起，那么很多中国人还是会买的，到那时候把衣服晾在外面就变成过去的风景了。人们会想要其他家用电器也靠替代能源如太阳能和风能发动，这样的需求使得企业加大研发力度，瞄准广泛的家用电器市场，以满足中国消费者的需求。（同时中国也会出口这些产品到那些要求低成本的国家。）

没有了能源枯竭和高成本用电的后顾之忧，中国人就能够选择在厨房里放烤箱来替代今天大多数人使用的煤气炉。中国人可以不用去餐厅和面包店就能享受到自家厨房里做出来的新品种。

洗碗机的普及需要一点文化上的转变，可能要稍晚一点才能引进中国人的厨房。在美国，洗碗机也花了一段时间才变得流行起来。因为美国人，特别是50和60年代的家庭主妇，不想表现得太懒，明明可以自己轻松完成的工作为什么要用机器来做呢？

不过，随着人们从贫穷或者低收入的打工族步入到中产阶级，他们都想纵容自己一下，买很多他们未必需要，但是会令他们的生活过得更加舒服的商品，除此以外，他们还可以跟朋友和邻居攀比。（在英语，这叫做"向邻居看齐"[keeping up with the Joneses]，"Jones"在美国是一个普通的姓，它的意思是，你比你的邻居拥有更多他们没有的东西，你就比他们更特别。）

不管怎样，我相信随着时间的推移，以及取之不尽的成本更低的能源的普及，很多中国人会开始愿意用像洗碗机那样的产品，因为这会给他们的生活带来更多便利和舒适。

  餐厨垃圾处理器则另当别论。

  餐厨垃圾处理器是一部机器，它可以把剩余的饭菜磨碎并冲到下水道里面。它安装在洗手盆下面，直接跟水槽连接上。水起到润滑作用，使得研磨器更好地工作，那些残羹剩菜就好像脏水一样随着水槽冲到下水道里。

  在美国，这为人们提供了便利，同时也解决很多公共卫生问题。

  没有吃完的食物和厨房垃圾，比如骨头，会招惹一些小动物去翻，寻找它们能吃的东西。这样就大大增加了老鼠的数量。老鼠携带的疾病可以传染给别的动物，特别是宠物猫和狗。这些疾病还可以通过直接和间接接触传染人类，猫和狗在外面感染病菌后，回家把病菌通过间接接触传染给人类。

  在美国，尽管我们还有鼠患和疾病，但我们已经把由老鼠传染的疾病发生率控制到很低，因为我们切断了它们的食物来源，剩下很少或没有食物在垃圾堆里面。

  我相信一旦这种餐厨垃圾处理器广泛应用于中国普通家庭的厨房水槽里，所有城市的老鼠数量会大大降低，环境卫生会有很大的改善，从而提高公共卫生水平。

随着替代能源的发展和应用,这一切都能够并且将会发生,我们地球最终会放弃使用日益减少的石油资源。

一个毋庸置疑的事实是:全世界的石油储备快要用完了。

问题是没有到*每一滴石油都卖出去*,那些西方石油公司是不会让新能源技术跟他们竞争甚至取代石油的。等到他们所有的石油都卖光了,他们就会公布早已研发出来只是一直没有公开的新能源技术。

在 90 年代末,通用汽车公司已经研发出一台纯电动汽车,并且已经通过试验和完善,少量地试水市场。可是当美国人开始大量需求这种车时,通用汽车则受到西方很多石油公司的压力而停止了这款车的生产。

每个购买了这款车的消费者都给予正面评价,越来越多的人准备买电动车,准备换掉石油发动机,汽油价格高,污染大,各种由石油引起的世界争端,都促使人们支持电动车,但是通用汽车却停止了电动车计划。它撒谎说这个新技术有缺陷,还没有充分做好进入市场的准备。(如果你想了解整个事件的来龙去脉,可以找一部名叫*谁消灭了电动车?[Who Killed the Electric Car?]*的记录片看,里面有很详细的说明。)

如果你想进一步证明世界的石油储备是不是快没了,你可以看一下目前的石油产业,当然那些石油公司会说一切都很好。

那些用来运油的油船都在老化,是时候换新的了。在正常情况下,像石油业这样的行业,每次靠这些油船把他们的产品送到客户手中,购买新的油船也很正常。但是,油船不但价格不菲,还需要制造很长时间。这些公司都知道,等到新的油船建好,早已经没有油可运了,因此,他们宁愿省了这一笔,继续用这些破破烂烂的油船。

**

替代能源的发展有一段有趣的历史值得中国人注意。

在 1980 年代,美国曾经是太阳能技术的领跑者。

不幸的是,美国已经被亿万富翁和他们的公司控制很多年了。在 80 年代,当时的美国总统罗纳德·里根(Ronald Reagan)听了石油巨富的命令,不再资助当时研发先进太阳能应用技术的公司,很快这些公司就倒闭了。过了一段时间,到了 90 年代,世界太阳能研究中心就转移到德国的公司去了。

请记住这一点,德国不仅仅是欧洲经济最强大的国家,它还一直受到同盟国,特别是美国的帮助。二战把德国几乎完全摧毁,美国想要帮助德国重建经济。(日本也有相同情况,这也是为什么日本在 70 到 80 年代大量往美国出口很多商品的原因。)

我不清楚从什么时候开始,大概是 1990 年代末到 21 世纪头十年的时间,中国成为了世界太阳能研究领域的领跑者。

我相信中国的做法很明智,这会加快中国成为有影响力的世界领袖的步伐。我相信随着更多太阳能和其他再生能源的使用,如风能和水能,中国能够靠自己彻底解决能源短缺问题,为所有中国人提供足够的能源。

到时候,所有家用电器都有足够的能量驱动,人们就可以无后顾之忧地放心购买这些消费品。

这也使中国能够从那些永无休止的世界争端中抽离出来,比如中东问题,以及其他世界各国企图控制石油产区而引起的争议和战争。

在我居住的这个中国地区,当穿梭于高速公路之间时,我不时看到很多屋顶上都装有太阳能热水器。我多么希望我的祖国也是这样。

中国还有美国没有的高铁。这也是另一个迹象表明美国在衰落而中国在向前发展。

另外，很多路灯是太阳能灯。

在2012年的伦敦奥运会上，新的技术也被使用。一款新型的人行道上铺的瓷砖可以感应人在上面踏步，把人行走时产生的动能转化为电能。

试想一下，每天有那么多人在世界各大城市的街道上行走，各国的政府如果没想到把这一项技术应用起来，那真是太愚蠢了。它尤其适合像中国这样多人的国家，人们不用多做什么，只是做每天他们都要做的事情——走路，就可以创造电力。

从我对中国的理解，我敢打赌，不久的将来我们就会看到这项技术应用到中国的人行道上，超过10亿人口产生的能量会大大减少中国对进口石油的需求，同时增加中国的能源储备。

风力涡轮机这项新技术也会（并且将会）很好地解决中国能源短缺问题。

当新的、大量的、成本更低的替代能源解决了中国的能源问题，能够满足中国庞大人口对能源的需求，中国也就毫无障碍地跃居成为21世纪的全球领袖。

中国通向未来的路障

我们都知道没有事情是完美的。尽管中国已经露出成为世界领袖的苗头，但这个国家还有很多国际性障碍需要克服。

我不停地告诉我的中国朋友，中国制造业最大的问题是质量控制问题。

在今天，基本上所有在这个地球上售出的商品都是中国制造的，当然除了美国自己大量生产和销售的炸弹、子弹、香烟和烈酒。

正是因为每件东西都是中国制造，一旦产品有什么问题，或者消费者投诉次品，美国公司都会利用产品都在中国生产的事实，把责任转嫁到中国头上。

我不喜欢唐纳德·特朗普（Donald Trump），这已经不是什么秘密。我认为他做人不道德，应该受到谴责，他是美国反华思想的鼓吹者。尽管他有估计 940 亿美元的身家，他还是设法宣布破产四次，多亏了美国的破产法，倾向美国富翁和他们的企业，牺牲了国家和人们的利益。正因为他有花不完的财富，他的名字已经成为一个品牌。他还有属于自己的电视节目，在节目中他会从一群想成为他一样的恶棍的人当中挑选一名做他旗下公司的执行官，向他学习，继承他的衣钵。他高傲自大，仅仅因为自己有钱并且能赚很多钱。他经常在美国公众面前出现，从来不会犹豫或错过任何一个责怪中国的机会，把很多美国问题算在中国头上。

尽管他说了很多中国的坏话，但都不影响他利用中国的廉价劳动力，制造唐纳德·特朗普名牌领带，然后以高价格卖给美国人，从中获得暴利。毕竟，他爱美国，谴责中国，但他不会给美国人工作，因为这意味着他要付给他们比中国工人多得多的薪水。

现在让我来告诉你们事实的真相。

企业想要最大化盈利，必须严格控制成本，他们用最差的原材料，用最廉价的劳动力，并且/或者给代加工厂施加压力，用尽方法压缩成本。正因为这些做法，生产出来的产品自然就质量不过关。不过美国公司不在乎这些，因为他们可以，而且一直都是，把质量问题责怪到中国头上。而中国工厂向来是任劳任怨，哪里有消费者投诉，他们就改进哪里。

丑陋的事实是，即使美国自己生产这些东西，同样的质量问题还是会出现在美国身上，因为那些压缩成本的举措无论如何都会妨害生产并导致质量下降。

可是记住这一点，目前其他国家人们使用的产品是中国生产的，抱怨中国是合情合理的做法。它直接影响了中国，中国工厂和工人的声誉。

**

　　另一个中国和西方国家之间的争议就是国际法律。在美国以及其他国家，财产权是法律给予保护的重要权利。这些权利包括知识产权和发明创造的权利，在不同领域有版权，商标和专利。

　　很多西方国家和企业都为中国企业和工厂侵犯他们的财产权而生气。中国公司肆无忌惮地拿来一个产品，复制一模一样的，拿出去当自己的卖。西方国家和企业之所以不敢把他们新的产品和概念带到中国来，这是部分原因。

　　我无意教中国企业如何做生意，我只是想说这是中国企业和工厂必须引起注意的问题。虽然我觉得这是个严重的国际性问题，但我想中国有能力在不久的将来自己解决它，如果我对中国未来的看法是正确的话。

　　今天，中国的商业和制造业不用太在意外国人对中国的负面看法，甚至国际法律也没有对中国产生太大影响。在将来，我相信中国人侵犯的将不再是外国人的版权、商标和专利，而是复制其他中国人的创意和发明。用另一句话说，当这些知识产权争端转向国内的发明者、公司和企业时，那么中国的法律必然会作出反应，制定更加严厉的干预手段来解决这些问题。

同样，当中国的工厂为国内消费者生产产品时，质量问题就会得到解决。中国消费者会要求更高质量的产品，那些顺应消费者需求生产出高质量产品的工厂，在 14 亿人口的庞大消费市场下，必定会走向成功。那些还在生产质量低下产品的工厂自然地很快会被淘汰。

世界的未来

自古以来，所有的技术和发明，从原始工具到现代武器，到 iPad 还有其他，都为了一个目的，满足人们的需要，这个需要可以是生存需要，也可以提供生活便利和娱乐活动，令人们更加快乐地活下去。

1870 年代的工业革命使人们步入了现代化进程；经历了第二次世界大战后，1957 年，苏联发射人类史上第一枚人造卫星，宣告航空时代的开始；随着计算机的发明，人类迫不及待地进入一个新纪元。在英语里，人们发明了很多不同称谓来形容这个历史上的新时期。它可以叫做科技时代（Age of Technology，Technological Age），计算机时代（Computer Age）或者数字化时代（Digital Age）。

不管怎么叫，先进技术不会停滞不前，而是快速地向前进步和发展。

我在 2001 年时以半价买了一台笔记本电脑，因为这台电脑已经过时，所以搞促销。当时放在我那台电脑旁边的另一台笔记本，是最新款，有更大的存储空间，运行速度是我这台的两倍。这意味着科学技术发展如此迅猛，当货架上的商品还没有卖出去，新的型号已经设计和研发出来，批量生产，并运到同一家商店的货架上，使得没有卖出去的商品变得过时，只能降价促销。

不过这至少让消费者能够以很低的价钱买到比较新的产品。

我重复又重复地跟做生意的中国朋友说，一定要紧紧跟着时代的步伐，与最新的趋势、技术和研究课题同步。

企业生产的商品始终要符合消费者的需求，新的点子和新的消费品趋势，都可以指引企业走到正确的路上。当一种消费品开始流行起来，又不至于太早过时，众多企业就会利用这个趋势，竞相生产同一类商品，尽可能地瓜分这个庞大的市场蛋糕。

请记住这一点，如果一个趋势延续下去，它总会达到一个点，过了这个点这个趋势就变成一个消费习惯。这个点什么时候发生，为什么发生，什么情况下发生，都没有确切的说法，但是很多消费习惯的形成是由于某种新产品的购买越来越流行，最后变成习惯，而这个产品往往是新的发明创造带来的。历史上出现了很多非常有创意的点子和产品，他们变得非常流行，非常有利可图，为生产企业带来了丰厚的利润。

为了能在新产品带来的市场蛋糕里分到一块，成功的企业领导者必须想得比别人快一步。具有创意的点子和新技术，符合消费者需求，为一些人带来巨大的财富，他们是苹果公司的史蒂夫·乔布斯（Steve Jobs，已经在下滑了），微软的比尔·盖茨（Bill Gates），和亚马逊的杰夫·贝索斯（Jeff Bezos）。

记住这个事实，这里有两个截然不同的条件。其中一个是，成功的企业家几乎必须能够预测未来。

这个说法毫不夸张，它并没有像你听到的那样难，特别是对于那些通晓很多不同领域学科的人来说，预测未来只需要以创造性思维作基础，加上正确的信息。事实上，时刻探索和发现这个疯狂世界上所发生的事情，同时留意在科学技术、农业、医药和其他领域的最新研究成果，对预测未来至关重要。

掌握了正确的信息，企业家和商人*可以*预测未来。

第二个条件是，有超前想法和创造力的企业家和商人不但可以很好地预测未来，他们还有丰富的想象力去创造他们的未来。

他们会首先发明有创意又符合实际需要的产品，这种产品能引起购买潮流，于是更多的企业加入这个市场，更多的消费者想要购买这种产品，于是它就顺理成章地变成一种消费习惯，人们离不开这种产品。

　　他们也会把目光转向已有的产品和购买潮流，利用他们创造性和超前性的思维方式，增加一些有创意的设计和产品，使原来的潮流更新颖和更激动人心。

　　记住这一点，没有人能准确具体地预测未来，可是，如果一个人了解足够多的历史、文化、科学技术、心理学和人类本性方面的知识，知道人们都想要什么，梦想什么，那么他就很容易预言未来某一方面的发展方向，以及人们对新的观点、发明和产品的接受程度。同时，知道人们的需求是如何被新的更有创意的产品所满足，他就可以更容易地创造未来。

　　我是星巴克的忠实粉丝，这个也不是什么秘密。（最令我感到意外的是，在美国最好卖的一款白巧克力摩卡，不知道是什么原因，竟然没有在亚洲市场上出现。还有他们不回复消费者的反馈邮件。）不管怎样，中国的企业家们可以向星巴克学习，学习它是如何发展壮大，如何进行品牌开发，还有怎样迎合消费者的需求，更重要的是如何引导消费者的需求到自己开发的产品上来。

当星巴克刚刚成为全美知名品牌时，很多美国人会被咖啡的价格吓一跳。这里有两点原因，一是他们的咖啡质量高，味道比市场上一般牌子的咖啡，以及其他咖啡厅卖的要好喝，二是他们营造的环境，给进来喝咖啡的人带来放松和喜悦感。

因此，尽管他们产品的价格要贵一些，但消费者还是愿意给这一笔钱。

此外，星巴克的领导层密切留意消费者的需求和购买习惯，总是设法满足他们的需求。举个例子，人们在家里也煮咖啡，这部分咖啡市场已经发生改变，趋向一次只煮一杯咖啡的产品。

在美国传统家庭里，总是喜欢一大早煮一壶咖啡来送早餐。甚至有些人只喝咖啡。可是一壶咖啡往往只有一到两杯会被喝掉，剩下没有喝的都要倒掉，这样显得很浪费。再加上，咖啡豆的价格越来越昂贵，这使得人们重新思考他们浪费咖啡的习惯。喝咖啡的人也偏爱*新鲜煮出来*的咖啡，不喜欢咖啡在壶里放很长时间。

解决办法是一次只煮一杯咖啡。

当一家公司开始设计和生产这样的机器时，人们很乐意地买了。"一杯咖啡"的市场，包括咖啡豆和咖啡机，很快就发展到一年 80 亿的市场份额。

星巴克看到了这一点,特别为这种广泛使用的一杯分量咖啡机提供合适的咖啡分量,选用上乘的咖啡豆,独立包装起来,方便使用。一年以后,星巴克宣布决定自己生产和销售这种一杯分量的咖啡机。

新技术的发展使得付款方式有了很大改变,人们可以通过手机上的应用程序简单快捷地付款。星巴克早在这项技术刚刚面世时就引进到其网站。

还有很多其他例子,说明了星巴克在商业运作中如何始终走在潮流的前端。正因为这样,我总是鼓励那些有前途的企业领导者多看看星巴克的历史,它的发展历程、品牌形象、市场策略以及它的全球视野,它是怎样演变成为国际上响当当的咖啡品牌,人们宁愿走出家里享受星巴克特别贵的咖啡,也不愿在家煮现成的普通咖啡。

我还是亚马逊的忠实粉丝,这家公司也是一个值得学习的例子,特别是它在消费者市场中表现了前瞻性视野。

杰夫·贝索斯早就知道网上购物只会发展越来越快,并且会占据全球市场更巨大的份额,他也足够聪明地早早就占了便宜。

他独创性地想到在网上售书,这个聪明绝顶的主意给亚马逊带来数十亿美元的入账。

从表面上看他的成功似乎是很简单的事情，贝索斯还做了一些关键性的有长远目光的决定，造就了今天的亚马逊的成就和辉煌，同时也给他带来巨额财富，成为全球富翁之一。

一开始，贝索斯注意到世界上有很多书店。而在美国，只有两家大公司在相互竞争。他还注意到虽然有很多书和出版公司，书店却始终受制于它的店面大小和库存数量。

而网络，却没有这样的限制。

网上书店基本上列出了所有出版商的所有书籍，顾客找起书来省时省力，还免了跑到书店的交通费用和时间。他们只需轻松地在网上下订单，亚马逊就会把书寄过来，产生的邮费远远低于亲自到书店跑一趟所需的交通费用和时间。

全新的售书模式使得亚马逊成为零售商的巨头。

然而，贝索斯并没有停在那里。他注意到在数字时代，人们可以很方便地从网上掌握新闻和其他信息，并且直接下载到他们的电脑中。

他能够想象得到，如果人们可以用电脑或者一个新的设备如电子书阅读器下载网上提供的书籍，那么印刷书籍的需求就会大大减少。

这样也节省了书籍印刷的成本，还有把纸质书运到读者手中的费用。

　　随着亚马逊 Kindle 电子书阅览器的发明，以及其他电子书阅读设备加入到这个竞争激烈的新市场，短短几年，亚马逊的电子书销售开始胜过印刷书的销售。现在，两种书的销量都在快速增长。

　　大家不要忘记在这段时期，新的科技成果不断得到应用，其中一个重要的改变就是所谓的"按需出版（print on demand）"。

　　在出版界，出版商要出版一个作家的书，必须印刷数千本，配送到各个书店里。如果这些印出来的书在书店卖不出去，必然占据书架的空间，最终难逃贱卖的命运。

　　现在，随着更先进更快的电子文档的应用，新的计算机操作的印刷机器已经研发出来，它可以读取任何格式的电子文档，只需向相连的计算机输入信息，印刷机就能生产出任意大小任意装订的纸质书。任何款式质地的封面都可以马上生产出来，不管是高级的真皮封面，还是便宜的纸质封面，又或是光滑的相纸封面。

　　贝索斯的其中一个建议是，亚马逊要开创属于自己的独特书店，这个书店采用了一种全新的书店经营模式。

这个书店会由图书展厅和咖啡厅两部分组成。所有书的样品会在书店里面展示，顾客可以亲眼看和用手摸各种图书的纸质、印刷效果和装订形式，从而选出一种心仪的印刷效果。

　　书店里同时配备了在线书籍目录查询，详细列出所有可供印刷的书籍的信息。

　　一旦顾客决定了买哪一本书，书店后台的大型印刷机器马上开始"制造"这本书，他们只需等待一杯咖啡或者一件小吃的时间，不出一个小时，就可以带着他们想要买的书离开书店了。

　　所有的书都可以马上印出来，他们再也不会被告知他们想要的书已经断货了。

　　这种新的经营方式给了贝索斯一些选择，他可以选择走不同方向的路，利用手上和公司的资金去开拓不同的业务。

　　贝索斯知道未来的零售书店将不再景气，网上书店才是主流，在他前瞻性的领导下，他决定放弃传统的砖头和水泥的实体书店，整合所有网络书店的资源和节省下来的成本，专注做电子书和他的 Kindle 电子书阅览器。

　　这个聪明绝顶的商业决定结果成为一个改变商业游戏规则的博弈术。

　　今天的亚马逊是目前为止最大的网络书店，在 2011 年，它的总收入达到 480 亿美元，其中一半归功于电影、音乐、电视节目、印刷书籍和电子书的销售。总体来说书籍比其他大部分亚马逊的产品都畅销，而电子书在那一半的份额里又占了很大一部分。

有一点需要补充，亚马逊的总收入中要拿出一部分作为广告费，给了另一个国际大公司——谷歌。

谷歌是西方国家最负盛名的搜索引擎。它主要靠出售广告来赚钱。可是，现在消费者已经不再需要在谷歌上搜素产品了，他们直接进入亚马逊网站寻找产品，一旦找到想要的，马上下单购买。

随着将来更多可能性不断出现，互联网商业的竞争必定越来越激烈。

*

当一个人考虑未来的发展，有很多不同领域需要考虑。

让我们先看看其中一个领域——如何把商品投放到市场中。

运输。

西方企业为取得最大利益，贪婪中国的廉价劳力而把工厂都搬到中国，尽管这意味着所有商品都要装上集装箱，放上轮船，漂洋过海送到国外的港口。

随着石油一天一天减少，由石油引起的全球性争议有增无减，石油价格不断攀升，远洋运输变得一个月比一个月贵。

最终，会有一个"转折点"的出现，那时候由廉价劳力省下来的钱，相比把商品从中国运到美国商店所需的高昂成本，显得不再重要。

今天，还有另外一个事实不能忽略，有权有势的企业已经有计划地对组织起来的工人发起攻击，削弱工会组织与雇主谈判的能力，这是美国史上从来没有发生过的。

美国工会势力强大，有组织工人的权力，这个组织为美国今天的繁荣作出了不可缺少的贡献。他们帮助建立了中产阶级，今天几乎所有税款都是中产阶级贡献的。工人们有工会做后盾，觉得自己的付出换来合理的报酬，工作更加顺心，生产力自然也提高了，同时他们也得到雇主的尊重。

美国一家汽车制造商的创立者亨利·福特（Henry Ford），引进了流水线的批量生产模式到美国的汽车制造业。他相信，工人们应该得到足够的薪水去支付日常所需，只有这样，才能提高员工士气，提高生产力，并且最终使公司走向兴旺。

今天的美国，（以及世界），跨国公司刚好把这个观念反过来。

美国企业正在试图利用那些渴望找到工作的失业者。尽管美国的生活水平相当高，甚至基本的主食也很昂贵，但很多没有工作的人仍然不肯屈服，不肯接受与中国工人一样的薪水。这些企业正在想尽一切办法，迫使美国人接受更低的工资。

这些公司，打个比方，假如明天成功迫使美国人接受低工资，那么他们会立即关掉中国的工厂搬回美国，同时省去了劳动力和运输两种成本。

还好这些都不怎么可能会发生，至少目前不会，这对中国和中国工人来说都是幸运的。

不容回避的事实是，当运输成本大过劳力成本时，企业会毫不犹豫地关掉中国的工厂返回美国，即使他们要给更高的工资，但是运输成本低了，他们还是会继续盈利。

石油起着至关重要的作用，但是不要忘记我们说过，对于将来，一切皆有可能。

货物放上货船或集装箱船，穿过海洋靠的是石油推动，在这以前，靠的是蒸汽，再之前，则是靠风力。今天，出于世界石油形势紧张，一些公司已经开始设计和建造现代帆船，这些船装有计算机操控的自动风帆，能够最大效率地利用风能。它同时还有一个小型发动机以备不时之需，不过大部分时间还是靠风帆，计算机能准确算出合适的角度抓住风力，这样运输货物到国外市场，就能大大节省能源，还保护环境。

今天还有高速铁路，火车跑得越来越快。中国是这方面的领跑者，在偌大的领土面积上输送着乘客在不同省市之间穿梭。

然而，今天的科技已经发展出比高铁更快的轨道。

新的技术已经实现火车在真空的轨道上行走，靠磁力驱动。如果这项技术应用到海底隧道，那么从美国到中国只需两个小时。

如果这项技术应用到货品运输上，它将改变国际贸易游戏的规则。到时候，货船也好，甚至节能帆船都会变得过时。在陆地，传统的铁路甚至货车都可以轻易地被这项技术所替代。

*

有时候，我们预测未来的发展，要彻底摒弃我们旧有的观念，接受现在的信息，这个对零售业的将来尤其正确。

目前在世界范围内零售业发生的一些变化足以引起店主的恐惧。这些变化叫做*展厅现象*（*showrooming*），它会持续下去，直到终结了我们今天熟悉的零售模式。

砖头和水泥的实体店就是不能与在线购物抗衡，这个是无法改变的事实。

实体店是具体的店铺，要用钱买下或租下来一个店面。开一家店，店主不但需要家具、陈列的商品、灯光、空调、收银机、销售人员，可能还要其他员工和一些管理人员。（在今天的商业气候下，经理们做得越来越少，工资却越来越高，而对公司贡献最大的工人却拿着最少的工资。）

基于这些运营开销，英语里面叫做*overhead*，实体店的价格是不可能跟网上商店的一样低。

这也是为什么今天在全球范围内的实体店店主都看到这么一种现象，很多客人走进实体店里寻找他们想要的，或者在广告上看到的商品，可是他们不会买，拿今天人人都有的手机拍张照，甚至还记下牌子和型号，然后若无其事地离开商店，回家，上网，以更低价格买到刚刚选中的商品。

随着这种现象发生得越来越多，很多实体店都会倒闭。这些门店如果只做公司的展示厅，里面销售的产品网上都有卖，它们是存活不下去的。

假如这种趋势继续下去，我相信它会，有可能我们今天所熟悉的购物环境会遭到彻底改变。

我不知道还要多长时间实体店就会完全被网店替代，如果没有其他特别事情改变我的预言的话，我也知道我是有一点前瞻过头了，但是到最后，我们可能在网上购买所有商品，唯一剩下的实体店将会是超市，那里有新鲜的水果和蔬菜，餐厅，专门店和便利店，卖那些我们生活不能离开的商品。

今天我们几乎可以在网上买到所有东西，可是快递需要时间。有一些产品，像牙膏、婴儿纸尿片、或者女性用品，如果在家用完了，人们等不及快递而要马上得到补给。

这会导致专卖这些急需品的社区便利店遍地开花。大部分这些便利店卖的很多商品都比大超市的贵，可是消费者还是愿意为*方便*多付那点钱，而不愿特意找一家购物中心或大型超市去买。因此，消费者很容易接受便利店的昂贵的价格。

不过，他们只会在便利店买那些他们临时用完，却没有在一周或一个月的网上采购中储备充足的物品。

很多便利店甚至可能有网店，提供邻近社区的送货上门服务。

在线购物成为主流也有好的一面，它会给运输和快递行业如联邦快递（FedEx）、DHL、UPS和顺丰快递等带来更多的机会。或者，如果你想加入这一行业，获得稳定和不断增长的收入，那么它也会给*你的*公司带来机会。

专门店会依然存在，不过它们可能以不一样的方式运行。

汽车经销商就是专门店的一个很好的例子。

在未来，如果人们还想买汽车，他们在买之前都想要亲眼看一下，摸一下，可能还想试驾一下。汽车不是人们会在网上购买的东西，他们都想要至少看一下真品。汽车经销商还是需要砖头和水泥的实体店，给顾客亲自看一看。不过他们可能不会在店上有完整的库存。他们只会展示样品车和试驾车，他们还可能会接受顾客的预定，按需要生产汽车。

把生产出来的商品放在货架上等待客人的购买其实是很低效的做法，不过目前这是我们做生意的方式。我相信只要生产者和消费者的一些观念加以改变，再加上先进技术的推动，假以时日，这种方式会有所改变。大部分产品会按需生产，小批量生产，而不是成千上万地生产。

在一些情况下，制造业不依赖机械而是工人生产产品，有利于工人严格控制质量，按比较小的数量生产产品。换一句话说，未来让工人生产产品会比用大型商业化机器人更符合实际需要，因为到时就不是像现在这样大规模生产了，这对工人都很有好处的。

像汽车这样的商品，给人们上门看车的展厅还是要有的，但经销商可能也会有网店，顾客可以在实体店看了，拿定主意后在网上购买。这个会引起经销商网店之间的竞争。它同时还会改变人们买车的考虑因素，为了提高销量，经销商必须降低价格或者提供折扣。

不要忘记了，一个有展厅的汽车经销商老板还要跟一个没有展厅只有网店的老板竞争，只有网店的老板的优势是他可以把车卖的更便宜，因为他没有展厅的支出，换言之，就是他的运营开销相对小一点。

未来化的汽车经销商，它不用展厅只有网店也可以把车卖出去。举个例子，经销商的老板可以把一些车开到大街上，在车身上贴满网站的广告。他也可以把车停在餐馆集中的地方，展示和推销他的产品。他还可以随时向有兴趣的客人提供试驾。你再读下去，就会了解到为什么有那么多的餐馆供他们停放在附近。

人们如果愿意，可以去看，去摸，然后在网上购买。

*

无论什么时候我跟我的朋友讨论这些未来的设想，他们都认为消费者无论如何都想要摸一摸产品再购买，因此实体店不会消亡。

我不同意。

如果我们按照今天的行事方法，在今天科技允许的情况下，我就同意。但是，我们谈论的是明天,是将来。想当年汽车刚刚发明时,也有很多人说,我们会一直骑马来代步,那个疯子的新发明不会代替马匹。好吧,今天马还是有人骑,可是没有人会骑马去上班或者去超市。

以今天的科学发展程度,我们还需要去商店,试衣服和鞋子,就为了摸一摸商品,感觉一下质地,因为我们害怕在网上买这些东西。

而这正是可以由先进的科学技术改进的东西。

随着科技的发展,消费者的心态也会随之改变。

当网上购物刚刚兴起时,很多人害怕泄漏他们的信用卡信息,事实上网上盗窃信用卡和身份信息的例子也很多,可是日益完善的科技使得网上购物越来越安全,现在已经成为很多人的购物习惯。

今天,人们可以在网上买到不同的标准尺寸,小码、中码和大码。

有钱人会走到裁缝店,量身定做他们的衣服。

今天的商品生产技术需要跟上科学技术的发展,顾客输入他们具体的衣服尺寸,就会得到合适大小的衣服,今天在一些网店已经做到这一点。可是没有多少网店可以提供标准规格以外的尺寸,一旦更多的顾客要求个性化的尺寸而不是这种通用尺寸，商店就会推出适应顾客需求的这种量身定做的衣服。

有了科技的帮助，加上网络销售的推动，这种个性化规格很快就会普及起来。

随着科技的发展，我们迈进新的时代，很多消费观念和态度会改变，一体通用的衣服规格将会很容易就过渡到个性化规格，无论贫富，大家都可以穿上量身定做的衣服。

随着制造技术的进步以及全新的网络销售和购买概念，它终究会发生。我不是说它可能发生，我是说它一定会发生。

在不久的将来我们将会用到 3D 全息影像技术进行网上购物。用户可以在一个电脑软件上输入他们的身体围度，接下来一个全息图像就会呈现出来，用户可以在图像上*试穿*各种他们喜欢或想买的衣服。女性用户尤其会爱上这项技术，因为她们可以从任意角度看到自己穿上衣服的效果，然后再决定购买。

而这一切都能在家里方便地做到，人们坐在电脑面前，喝着喜欢的饮品，悠闲地试穿衣服，不再需要浪费时间一家一家服装店寻找合适的衣服。

科技正在一如既往地改变我们的生活，并且还会继续改变下去。

其中一种在将来存活下来的砖头和泥土的实体店，就是餐馆。

人类是社会动物。我们喜欢跟朋友和家庭聚在一起。我们还喜欢吃。我们特别喜欢跟朋友和家人一起吃东西！

我们特别喜欢在餐厅吃饭，因为这样我们就不用做饭，把厨房弄脏，再花时间弄干净，吃完还要洗碗，刷盘子。

餐馆，还有提供社会聚会的商业活动和场所比如剧院、演唱会或者夜总会等，都会在将来继续繁荣兴旺下去。

超市也会继续存在。一些超市会推出在线购物和送货上门。我相信大部分人会继续在超市买新鲜食品，像水果、蔬菜、鱼类、肉类、鸡蛋和类似他们可以自选的东西。

除了去超市买东西，社交活动会成为人们离开家里，出去市区的最主要原因，其中下馆子占了很大一部分。

这同时也会引起餐饮业的一些变化。他们之间的竞争会加大，顾客会有更丰富的选择。

在今天的商业环境下，人们会很小心地选择餐馆的类型和地址。例如，在一家印度菜餐馆旁边再开一家印度菜餐馆是不明智的。同样道理也适用于比萨，泰国菜或者其它任意类型的餐馆。

聪明的餐厅老板可能会把同类型的餐厅设在同一个社区或同一条街道，距离足够远，这样才可以避免跟同类餐厅竞争。不过在将来，这一情况会改变。

在将来，由于没有了服装店，鞋店和玩具店这样的商店像今天那样隔开不同的餐馆，更多的餐馆会挤在一起，相互挨着，这样同类风格的餐厅就难免要隔得很近了。

这样会加大餐馆之间的竞争。

同时，餐厅会开始把窗户的位置卖给其他经营衣服、电脑或者手机的人，让他们把商品展示在窗户旁，这样，客人吃饭时、等位时，或者走过路过就会顺便看看这些商品。很多餐厅会生意很好，客人需要等位的情况很常见。他们在等位时肯定要做些什么，这时正好可以看看这些广告。

在餐厅橱窗上打广告，无论对餐厅还是这些网络销售公司，都是双赢的策略。

餐馆和网络销售公司可以相互合作。餐厅可以给顾客派发折扣代码，顾客上网购买产品时有折扣，同时在网店消费的顾客又可以拿到该餐馆的优惠代码，享受折扣的食物和饮品。

在未来网上购物的大潮中，能够生存下来的实体店不多。餐厅和网店的紧密合作开启了新的、更富有创意的市场营销和推广渠道，共同分享未来的消费市场。

未来的趋势是，所有东西都会在网上销售，除了卖新鲜食品的超市、起展示厅作用的实体店销售像汽车这样的商品、还有社区里面的便利店和餐馆，很难再找到卖其他商品的实体店了。

请不要忘记，我在这里只说近期未来的可能性。我之所以强调近期，是因为我知道目前新的点子每天都在转化成新的发明和创造，而一些新的卓越的发明会改变我们所知的一切。

总的来说，科技是个好东西，它可以使人类社会变得更加美好。然而有时候，它又可以毁掉一切。

不管科技是好是坏，新的事物每天都在发明，"好"和"坏"的关键在于我们如何利用它。我只能希望新发明的科技会治好生病的地球，促进社会和谐和世界和平，解决很多由疾病、贫穷、饥饿以及无家可归引起的问题。

我们将拭目以待。

中国的未来

章家敦（Gordon Chang），备受尊重的美国律师，他经常出现在美国新闻和评论节目中。在2001年，他写了一本书名为《中国即将崩溃》（*The Coming Collapse of*

China），他断言，基于很多原因，中国的经济将会在 2006 年崩溃。显然，他错了。这正是中国在世界崛起的时期，也是作为中国人的骄傲时期。

那些美国和跨国企业贪婪地利用中国及中国廉价劳力，把中国推向一个繁荣的位置，远远领先世界上其他地区。当其他国家面临严重的金融问题时，中国却富饶和兴旺。

美国的企业不顾已经把美国经济搞的一团糟的事实，继续转移美国工厂到中国来。他们的贪婪和追求廉价劳力的愿望超过其他一切因素。他们早就知道他们会摧毁美国经济，夺走很多美国人的工作机会，最终导致国力衰落，把中产阶级推向贫穷，但是他们不在乎。他们只知道十多亿中国人迫切需要工作，哪怕工资低到在美国人眼里是*奴隶工资*（slave wages）。在英语里这个词有双关语的意味，因为奴隶本来是不用给工资的。

美国企业的这些做法其实是为了寻求短时间的高利润回报，牺牲了长远的经济利益和国家稳定。这不但对美国和美国工人不利，长远来讲对企业本身也是自掘坟墓。

可是这一切对中国、中国人民特别是中国的工人们都是非常有好处的。

实际上，美国企业关闭美国的工厂而转移到中国，正是中国成为 21 世纪全球领袖的最主要的原因。

在二战结束时，美国是世界的工厂。今天，中国是世界的工厂。正因为这样，靠着 80 年代末以来从西方国家手中积攒起来的财富，中国进一步得到发展和充实。今天的中国，富裕、繁荣和零债务，相比之下，其他国家却处于严重的经济下滑，连路桥和电网的建设，以及帮助穷人和老人的社会福利项目都不能顺利进行。

西方国家日益衰退，中国却靠贸易出口推动经济繁荣，这些因素都必然促进中国崛起成为世界霸主。

既然世界上大部分人都是拿着低工资的穷人，那么更多的工作机会和持续上涨的工资会大大增强国家和个人的财富。个人财富的积累会促进中产阶级的形成。中产阶级的壮大又会促进国家的繁荣。当人们手中掌握更多的财富，有多余的可支配的收入时，他们会想买更多的东西，使生活容易些。如果每个中国人都买得起一辆车，谁还会走路或骑自行车上班呢？

当一个国家在世界各国中的地位有所上升，权力越来越大，它的人民自然也会经历生活质量的提高。生活质量的提高通常包括人们赚更多的钱，积累更多财富，买更多的商品来满足个人需求。

同时，这些因素相互依赖，相互促进，共同发展。

依靠生产力的提高，经济和出口的增长，还有中产阶级的壮大，一个国家人们的生活水平会跟着提高。部分是因为这个国家有足够的财富去建设或改善国家基础设施。新的道路、桥梁、电网、公共卫生设备、自来水净化、高铁、还有其他方面都会大大得益于国家经济的增长和财富的积累。此外，帮助穷人和老人的社会福利项目也会达到政府更慷慨的资助。

得益于一些世界事件和中国的制造业，今天的中国人很幸运地得到很多工作机会。在接下来的几年里，充足的工作机会将眷顾更多的中国人。

我生长在美国繁荣时期的尾声。读大学是一件很昂贵的事情，我必须赚足够的钱供自己上大学。正是因为我当时还处于美国经济繁荣阶段，我通常能够同时做两到三份兼职，这种情况一直维持了整个大学阶段。

这样的时期很快就会来到中国。由于有足够工作机会，很多人会选择打两份工，牺牲一些自己的业余时间，赚更多的钱。最终他们所赚的钱会把他们带进日益壮大的中产阶级。

今天，中国大约有 2 亿人挣的钱足够被认为是中产阶级。西方经济分析家们预言，到了 2025 年，中国会有 5.2 亿人成为中产阶级。

到了那个时候，我觉得这个数字可能有点低了。我认为中国的发展速度惊人，远远超过西方经济分析家们的预测。这意味着到时候，会有比他们想象的更多的中产阶级。

2011 年，中国的人均工资增长了 12.4%。工资还不够高，不过这已经是一个开始。去年，中国的经济总量超过日本，成为世界第二大经济强国。一些经济学家预言，在 2016 年到 2020 年之间，中国将超过美国成为全球经济总量最大的国家。就如二战后美国的中产阶级的工资为美国提供燃料，使其经济膨胀了三十年，中国庞大的劳动大军及其日益壮大的中产阶级会驱使中国在 21 世纪成为世界领袖。

终有一天，中国会彻底跑在西方国家的前面，尽管这未必对国际贸易和国际关系有好处。今天的中国不需要西方，西方却需要中国。

由于科技的发展，世界变得越来越小，国家之间的外交策略继续占据重要的位置。但事实是今天的西方国家需要中国的生产能力，并且在短时期内不能离开中国。这个已经使中国成为世界舞台上一个更加强大的国家。

我在2012年写这本书的时候，中国的制造业已经稍微下滑了。原因是明显的。西方国家没有钱了，他们很穷。他们被华尔街、跨国大银行和大公司制造的金融问题沉重地打击了。很多欧美国家的消费者已经改变购物习惯，只购买必需品。

这个趋势会继续下去，人们花掉更多的储蓄，为了生存借更多的钱，并且努力在失业或面临失业风险的情况下度日。

中国人的消费能力正在迅速提高。一部分是因为西方没有钱了，一部分是因为中国国内生活质量的提高，多亏了中国靠出口积累的财富。

中国消费型社会的形成正是西方国家和企业数年来朝思暮想的，就好像年轻男人梦想要娶电影明星为妻。

记住这一点，卖出尽可能多的产品是每个公司的梦想。如果他们能够卖出一个，他们会推销两个；如果他们卖出两个，他们会推销四个。不像大部分美国学校的学生们，美国企业擅长数学，他们知道美国只有3亿人。这意味着他们只有3亿潜在消费者。可是中国是市场潜力是14亿。

拿我的情况打个比方，如果有1%的中国人买我这本书，我就很高兴了。即使成本低，利润低，我也会为 1%的销售额感到非常高兴。

我打算以中英对照的形式出版这本书，这也是一个说明中国消费市场潜力的例子。我可以只发行中文版本，但是我知道，在今天的中国，会说和读英语的人，比美国人口还要多。是的，这已经是事实，超过 3 亿中国人说英语。（相比之下，我听说过，在美国，大概只有 2 到 3 个人会说中文，或者再保守一点，说 0-5 个人吧）（好吧，我的确是在开玩笑，不过会说中文的美国人真的很少。可是，那些聪明的人，知道中国正在崛起成为世界领袖的人，开始学中文了，并且保证他们的下一代也要学中文。）

尽管中国正迅速朝世界领袖的方向发展，但西方企业仍然觉得很难把他们的产品打入中国市场。一方面，西方企业不愿意在价格上妥协，他们不肯以相对低的利润卖他们的产品，尽管销售总量会是巨大的。但是最终会有一些进口产品，中国人愿意以高价格购买。

但是真正推进中国经济繁荣，极大地促进中产阶级成长的，将是中国企业为国内市场生产消费品。

当 14 亿中国人开始在工厂和公司赚到更高的工资，他们变成消费者，于是中国企业开始为 14 亿消费者生产产品，可想而知，到时中国的经济腾飞速度将会震惊世界。

到时，中国的工厂将会前所未有地加大生产力度，他们甚至要扩建或者增加临时厂房来满足国内消费者的需求。紧接着，更多需要工作的中国人会找到这些工厂，他们提供各种层次的工作，从低技术含量低收入的工种，到要求具备经验和知识，受过高等教育的高科技岗位。

不断增长的工资，加上由消费需求创造的不断增加的工作机会，会反过来创造更多的消费需求，范围涉及所有工厂生产的所有产品。

为了应付不断增长的订单，工厂要雇佣更多的工人，工资自然也会提高。

工资提高的过程将会是这样：两家工厂生产同一种产品，他们都试图紧跟消费者的需求来生产这种产品。一家工厂老板会意识到，如果其工厂的产量增加，或者工人的技术有所提升，那么其产品就会在市场上占有优势。于是，这个工厂就会稍微提高工人的工资，以吸引更多的工人过来，特别是有技术有经验的工人。

另一家工厂的工人会打听到，在竞争对手的工厂里，工人做与自己同样的工作，却比自己拿的钱多。于是他们当中的一些就会辞去这个工厂的工作，带着他们的经验去到工资高的工厂里面打工。

失去工人的工厂迫于无奈，只好也跟着提高工人的工资。

在一段时间里，由于中国消费者对产品的需求有增无减，工厂的利润持续上升，中国工人的工资也会不断上涨。

整个过程反复循环，不但促进中国经济迅速发展，还极大地扩充了中产阶级规模。

这是一个对所有人都有好处的局面，企业会获益，工人们会获益，国家也会获益。三方相互促进，共同增长。这时的中国是当年二战后美国经济繁荣的写照。

这时候另一个产品质量问题也会同时得到解决。

如今中国的一个重大问题是，西方企业要求产品以最低成本生产。而达到最低成本的唯一途径是减少原材料、劳力和生产环节的成本。于是中国制造的产品就挂上了质量不合格的恶名。

我不断提醒我的中国朋友，现在西方企业做的是，强迫中国厂家在节省成本的前提下生产出尽可能高质量的产品。这个当然不容易。有时候还不可能实现。

当次品充斥美国市场，人们抱怨产品质量时，你觉得美国企业会怪谁呢？当然是中国、中国工厂和中国工人。

在中国经济迅猛发展的情况下，这个问题会很容易得到解决。那些生产高质量产品的工厂满足了中国消费者的需求，他们继续生存下去，越做越大；那些生产低质量产品的工厂没有满足消费者的需求而遭淘汰。

*

整个过程会持续 20 到 30 年时间，中国经济迅猛发展，并且形成和壮大了一支令每个国家都羡慕的中产阶级队伍，正如 20 世纪美国的中产阶级也曾是其他国家羡慕的对象一样。中国会富裕得难以置信，把衰落的西方国家远远抛在身后，成为 21 世纪最强大的国家。

如果中国继续沿着这条路走，这是最可能会发生的结果，除非世界发生了不同寻常的事情，或者改变游戏规则的新科技出现使我的判断错误。

如果这真的是中国要走的路，在接下来的 30 或者 40 年，或者 40 年到 70 年或 80 年间，无论发生什么事情都是人们的猜想。然而，接下来的这部分则要说明一些可能出现的情况。

不太遥远的未来

如果历史的车轮继续沿着现在的轨迹前进，没有大的变故，那么中国应该走我所预测的跟美国一样的路。不要忘记，我并不是在预言，我只是在教你们一些20世纪的美国史，了解当时的美国是如何成为世界领袖，以及它的地位又如何在本世纪转移到中国身上。

如果没有大的变动，中国确实沿美国的足迹走下去，那么我就有理由相信，即使中国的技术处于领先优势，中国还是会重演美国在20世纪末21世纪初的衰落过程。

这意味着中国有大概60年或多或少的繁荣期，之后就会开始像美国那样走下坡路。

等到工资涨到一定程度，中国企业就会寻求成本更低的生产方式，同时跟上消费者需求。

可是谁知道在未来50年里科技会如何发展呢？新的科技，特别是即将来临的新科技，足以改变我所说的一切。

我经常深入思考很多事情，如果企业生产的产品没有人要，他们会怎么办呢？这是我一直关注的问题。

举个例子，越来越多的工厂开始用机器人生产，为此我感到忧虑。

现今社会，人们靠工作赚钱来购买生活必需品，最重要的当然是食物，此外生活必需品还有住房、衣服和必要的医疗。

当经济不景气时，人们自然会减少购买不必要的东西，只买必需品。

越来越多的工厂使用机器人替代劳动力，人们正在失去工作。目前为止这还没有成为中国的主要问题，然而其他国家的工人已经切身体会到它所带来的影响。

使用机器人和计算机辅助生产，的确给产量带来很大提高。

可是我不得不想到的问题是，如果人们没有工作，就没有收入，一个人没有收入来源了，不要说其他非必需品了，就算是食物这样的必需品也难以购买。

换句话说，工厂因为使用机器人替代工人而大大提高了产量，可是从长远来看，人们失去工作，没有收入来源，那些高效率生产出来的大量产品却没有消费市场。

人们怎么生存下去？他们怎样得到食物？他们用什么来得到或者"买到"食物？

我们可能需要完全改变我们的思维方式。我说的"我们"指的是全人类，不光是国家和政府。

我相信一些机器人能大大提高生产效率，但如果我们继续用机器人取代工人，不换一套现代社会的基本生存哲学，那么这将对全世界人民非常非常地不利。

以上我的观点值得深深思考。

从商业和贸易的角度看，这个问题变得更有意义和切合实际。如果所有产品都由机器人生产，工人数量锐减，谁会买这些产品呢？

这个道理看起来很简单，可是今天的企业为了短期的利益，宁愿继续以机器人替代工人，不顾长远利益。

另一个中国今天要面对的难题是与印度的竞争。

当中国成为世界领袖和消费型社会的时候，我相信这个问题会迎刃而解。

随着中国工资的上涨，一些中国的工厂可能会搬到印度，寻求更廉价的劳动成本。

他们这样做的原因与美国把工厂搬到中国如出一辙。印度有很多迫切需要工作的人，他们愿意接受很卑微的工资。

但是，印度生产的产品回到中国需要运费成本以及相关进口税费，这会附加在产品的成本上，提高产品的销售价格。

因此，聪明一点的做法是把工厂继续留在中国。

当然，如果中国企业生产的产品仍像今天一样以出口为主，那么从印度也可以把产品运到世界各国，这也是一个可能性。可是，像我一直预测的，一旦中国的消费市场成熟起来，中国将不需要出口产品。出口贸易只成为庞大的国内市场销售之外的一点点额外收入。

若一切如我所想，那么遥远的未来才是中国人们要注意的。

至于遥远的未来，那就更难预测了。

导致美国衰败的原因是1970年代工人的工资持平。当时的工资水平基本没有变化，但是物价水平却上涨了。企业生产的成本提高，为了获得相同的利润，他们也提高了商品的销售价格。

美国消费者受了两次打击。一是工资水平没有变化，实际上是变相减少了。二是物价水平持续上升。

一开始它导致了更多的家庭主妇出来工作，因为一个家庭光依靠父亲的薪水已经难以维持，必须靠两个人的收入。

接下来银行设置了圈套，推出更容易贷款的信用体制。为了弥补少了的薪水和上涨的物价，美国工人们上当了，借了银行很多钱，变得欠债累累。

那些银行、华尔街股市和大公司财团对政府影响太大，他们控制政府，美国工人和消费者只能做砧板上的鱼肉任他们宰割，欠债太多以至到了 2012 年还不能恢复过来，甚至恢复的希望都看不到。

我只能希望中国的法律会对大企业有所控制，希望中国人从美国的错误中学到经验，不要允许这样的悲剧发生在中国人身上。

让我们把目光再放远一点，如果成为世纪领袖后的中国真的同美国一样走下坡路，那么最大的威胁可能会来自非洲。

这也是一个可能性（我不是说很大的可能性，因为太远的未来不好预测），如果中国高度复制我在这本书里形容的美国走过的路，那么未来的中国企业就会停止增加工人的工资，开始把工厂搬到非洲，那里也有很多穷人急切想要工作，接受比未来中国工人低很多的薪水。

有一件事非常肯定——以我现在的年龄，是不可能看到将来我的预测是对是错了。

不过谁知道呢？新技术有可能在我活着的时候就研发出来，把我们的寿命延长 50 或者 100 岁也说不定。

中美合作

关于中美关系，我有一点话要说。

我相信美国和中国能够保持良好的朋友关系，并且将来在任何情况下都能继续保持良好的朋友和伙伴关系。我相信中美文化有很多可以相互借鉴的地方。

　　可是，在世界历史上，任何两个国家之间的关系几乎都只有两种可能：朋友或者敌人。

　　如果美国和中国成为敌人，对两个国家都是毁灭性的影响，对整个世界的影响也难以想象。

　　如果成为朋友，两个国家的文化和创造力合在一起可以对世界和人类的发展产生难以估计的贡献。

　　为了整个世界和两个国家的利益，我希望我们保持友好关系。

　　我可以一一列举可能引起两个国家间问题和争端的原因，但这本书不是关于这个，也不是关于政治。这本书是关于商业、中国以及中国在本世纪将成为世界领袖的过程。

　　为了将来全世界和人类的利益，我希望美国和中国能保持友好和重要盟友的关系。这是我结束这一章时带着的唯一想法。

结语

我写这本书的其中一个原因是，我想帮助我那些辛勤劳动的中国朋友们，我相信他们值得拥有一个美好的未来。我更希望他们跟全世界辛勤劳动的人们一起奔向繁荣与昌盛的未来。

另一个原因是我的中国朋友们不是很了解美国历史。由于他们不了解20世纪的美国历史，他们不知道现在的他们在世界上有什么优势。很多国家失业率高企，中国的劳动力市场却供不应求，并且工资水平不断上升。中国掌握的财富越来越多，打下了坚实的经济基础，并带动国家基础设施迅速发展，用的是世界最先进的技术。庞大的人口基数已经不再是负担，而是经济发展的最大优势。

谁都不能准确预见未来，但有一点可以肯定，就是我们正处于一个激动人心、有着无限可能、却又危险的时期，似乎什么事情都有可能发生。

如果世界沿着它现在的道路继续前进，我相信我在这里所说的一切都极有可能发生。

可是，不要忘记，这只是一个笼统的观点。中国应该循着与美国相似的路继续走下去，当然一切皆有可能，不寻常的事情时有发生，例如：第三次世界范围的战争，中国也难以幸免；中国、亚洲、甚至世界性的环境灾难；全球性流行病；影响到每一个国家的经济灾难；甚至外星人入侵地球，小行星撞击地球并引起物种灭绝，就像6500万年前恐龙灭绝的情况一样。我相信所有这一切都有可能发生。

不过如果社会保持这样的状态继续前进，抛开一切由新科技或我在这里提到的原因引起的变动，中国将会占尽天时和地利的优势。

这里有几点要记好：如果任何一些我预测的情况实现，中国如我所言成为世界霸主，那么中国人要感谢美国的亿万富翁和他们的公司，是他们摧毁美国经济和工会组织，控制美国政府制定倾向他们那一阶级和企业的法律，他们伤害了我们国家、人民和美国经济的利益（同时也伤害了其他国家人民的利益，破坏地球环境）。他们，美国的亿万富翁及其企业，是中国今天取得的地位和成就的原因，也是中国成为"世界工厂"的原因，是中国出口型经济繁荣的原因，是中国即将加入发达国家行列，崛起成为世界领袖的原因。

他们是美国衰落的主要原因。

在西方有一则寓言叫做《蝎子和青蛙》。蝎子想要过河，但它不会游泳，于是叫青蛙帮忙背它过河。青蛙告诉蝎子，它不想背蝎子过河，因为青蛙知道蝎子会蜇它并且杀死它。蝎子声称这是很愚蠢的行为，因为青蛙死了的话，不会游泳的蝎子也会淹死。最后，青蛙同意背蝎子过河。为了让蝎子安全地保持在水面上，青蛙努力地往后蹬。等到河过了一半，青蛙感觉背上有刺痛感，它转过头去，看见蝎子正把它的毒针从青蛙背上拔出来，青蛙感到它的手和脚开始麻木，再也不能游泳了。青蛙问蝎子为什么要这样做，蝎子明知道这样大家都会同归于尽。蝎子说，"这是我的天性啊。"

美国企业就像那只蝎子，而美国人民就像那只青蛙，在经济景气时，美国人民也是他们的工人和消费者。与原来故事不同，美国工人、以及买他们产品的美国工人阶级和中产阶级消费者万万没有想到，企业有钱了以后就不顾国家和人民利益，拼命追求自己的利益最大化。就好像蝎子最终露出了本性一样，美国企业的本性是寻求利益最大化，不断缩减成本和增加利润，却不管青蛙的死活，青蛙才是他们拥有今天成就的最大功臣。

沃尔玛这家公司就是那些具有破坏本性的大企业的一个最好的例子。我憎恨创立沃尔玛的沃尔顿家族。沃尔玛几乎在每个城市都建立了大规模的购物中心，他们还强迫政府给予资助建立他们的购物中心和道路，完全背离了资本主义的原则，他们还帮助自己的员工申请政府援助从而少给他们工资，这些政府援助项目本来是帮助低收入人群的，而这些员工都没有从沃尔玛得到足够工资。此外，沃尔玛及其持有者沃尔顿家族没有缴纳他们应该交的税款。最后还有，因为他们给中国工人的工资实在少得侮辱人，他们获得了极其巨大的收益。但是他们还不满足，他们还想要更多。

还有一点，在沃尔玛进驻的每一个城市，因为得到政府的资助以及从中国来的廉价产品，他们采购能力强，能够把商品的零售价压得很低，导致本地商店和企业根本无法与之竞争，最终走向倒闭。

从长远来看，他们终将会失去市场，因为越来越多的美国人停止购买他们不需要的东西，只买那些必需品如食物、基本的衣物和药品。

在沃尔玛的经营战略中提到，不但要把分店开到全球各个角落，不需注重忠诚消费群的建立，还要不断挤压其他竞争对手的生存空间，直到在同行里做到一枝独秀。一旦所有竞争对手都被它排挤，它就可以为所欲为，想开什么价开什么价，剩下的消费者也无从选择。

幸亏，这对中国不会是问题。中国正走在一条独立的不一样的路上。在我写这本书的2012年，中国制造业的放缓和一些西方客户的流失只是中国通向繁荣富强的路上小小的一块隆起的地面而已。

因此，随着许多美国和西方客户的流失，中国继续沿着它的道路走向繁荣和富强。在目前世界上所有国家当中，中国是唯一一个准备好接过美国手中接力棒的国家，它将迅速往前跑，畅通无阻地遥遥领先于其他国家。

因此，对我的中国朋友们，我要说，继续做好你手中的工作。不断学习，不断思考，不断提升自己，还要不断以崭新的、创意的眼光看待未来。你们占尽了天时和地利，正如英语里有云，*世界属于你的*（the world is your oyster）。接过接力棒往前冲吧。没有人可以阻你的路。

****

那些听不见音乐的人觉得舞者是疯子。
——*佚名*

***
附录 A:

商业理念：美国历史中关于二战后的经济繁荣时期，有很多故事和例子可以很容易地被中国所用，中国的企业家们要做的只是去发掘这些故事并且搬到中国来。

例如，美国有一些野心勃勃的自由职业者来到汽车经销商那里，不过他们没有买车或者租车，而是跟店主谈起生意来。他们说如果能够找到五个人同时租同一款车，店主要在租金上给予优惠，并且额外送给他一辆车。经销商们同意了，因为对他们来说这是个双赢的买卖——给一点优惠是可以实现的，就算要送出去一辆车，但租出去五辆车的利润还是不少（在美国，租车比买车的利润高很多）。就好像额外请了一个不需要给工资和福利的员工一样——那辆免费的车只相当于很低的佣金。于是这些目标明确的自由销售员就会去找医生、律师等各种不同职业的人，承诺给他们一款特定名车的出租价格优惠，并附带很多升级服务。他们可以一直找，直到同时有五个人愿意接受这项服务。最后经销商以小折扣同时租出去五辆车，那些自由销售员也拿到了一辆免费的车。

很多住在豪宅里的美国人实际上不用给租金，因为他们答应给这些有钱人管理他们的物业。这些有钱人要么就经常到处跑不在家，要么就只住其中一栋房子，想有个人也住住其它的房子，帮他们每天打理、清洁和收拾好，也可以防止有人闯入或者擅自居住，这样至少表面上这些房子每天都有人进出。

还有另一个例子，我不确定它是什么时候发生、由谁发起的，一些眼光独到的企业家足够聪明地利用中美文化差异来做生意：鸡爪。

据我所知，没有美国人吃鸡爪。在美国，如果我们买整只鸡，它是包装好的去头去脚卖的。家禽业过去索性把鸡爪扔掉。至于鸡头，不同地方有不同文化，但大部分美国人不喜欢在吃的时候，那个食物回过头来看他们，他们会感到害怕。

因此，我不知道从哪里、什么时候和如何开始，可是就是某个地方有人意识到中国人很爱吃有嚼劲的鸡爪。因此，与其扔掉，美国人想到把鸡爪卖给中国人，如今鸡爪成为美国出口中国的最多的产品之一。

换句话说，鸡爪在美国从毫无利润的垃圾摇身一变成为高利润的出口中国产品。

这里只是举几个例子说明有创意思维的生意点子，他们在中国也可以适用。

事实上尽管中美文化有差异,但是仍然有很多被美国文化证明可行的商品或商业点子是可以用到中国消费市场上的。

记住这一点,有创造力的思维和想法是最重要的。有了创意,就有无限的可能性。

任何人如果有兴趣跟我讨论这本书中提到的想法或者中国的未来,都可以联系我,我将会是你们的咨询顾问,我的电邮地址是:filosfrfrank@yahoo.com。由于我不会中文,中国读者请用英文咨询。可能性是无尽的,这样的讨论是有趣的,讨论的结果甚至能够带来巨额财富。

Acknowledgments from Translator:

I would like to thank Frank Silva, the author, who placed his faith in me and gave me the opportunity to translate his work. I admire his expertise in words, richness in life experiences and his creative thinking toward China's bright future. Every Chinese person should read this book, especially those who are thinking of moving abroad, it will give them confidence to live better lives in China.

~Tracy Lu, October 2013

The translator welcomes comments and discussion and can be reached at tracyindongguan@gmail.com

About the Translator
Tracy Lu has a bachelor's degree in Library Science from Changchun Normal University. She has been spending all her adult life learning English. She has worked various positions after college, including as an office worker in the public security bureau, as a manager of a Western restaurant and a teacher working with autistic children. She is now a professional translator and is in her third year as a Staff Writer for the local foreign-run English language magazine *Here! Dongguan*, where she uses her expertise in the English language for translation and interpretation. She loves the attention to detail necessary in translating between Chinese and English and values the insights into Western thinking that understanding English provides her.

感谢

在这里我要感谢这本书的作者 Frank Silva，谢谢他对我的信心以及给我这个机会翻译他的作品。对于他流畅的文笔、丰富的人生经历以及对中国光明前景的创新性思维，我深深感到佩服。我认为这本书对每个中国人都有用，特别是正打算移民出国的中国人更应该读一读这本书，它会增强我们过上美好生活的信心，相信中国前景是值得期待的。

FRANK SILVA

卢秀娟
2013 年 10 月

本书翻译欢迎读者的任何评价和建议，请发送到以下电邮地址：tracyindongguan@gmail.com。

关于翻译

卢秀娟，广东省东莞市人，长春师范大学图书馆学学士毕业。毕业后自学英语，目前在一家由以色列人创办的英文杂志《HERE! Dongguan》从事英语写作，同时从事中英翻译工作。

www.ingramcontent.com/pod-product-compliance
Lightning Source LLC
Chambersburg PA
CBHW071757200526
45167CB00017B/352